GACE English to Speakers of Other Languages (ESOL)

119 120 Teacher Certification Exam

By: Sharon Wynne, M.S.
Southern Connecticut State University

"And, while there's no reason yet to panic, I think it's only prudent that we make preparations to panic."

XAMonline, INC.
Boston

Library of Congress Cataloging-in-Publication Data

Wynne, Sharon A.
   English to Speakers of Other Languages: Teacher Certification / Sharon A. Wynne. -1st ed.
   ISBN: 978-1-60787- 063-0

1. ESOL   2. Study Guides   3. GACE   4. Teachers'
Certification & Licensure
5. Careers

Disclaimer:

The opinions expressed in this publication are the sole works of XAMonline and were created independently from the National Education Association, Educational Testing Service, or any State Department of Education, National Evaluation System or other testing affiliates.

Between the time of publication and printing, state specific standards as well as testing formats and website information may change. Such changes are not included in part or whole within this product. Sample test questions are developed by XAMonline and reflect content similar to real tests; however, they are not former tests. XAMonline assembles content that aligns with state standards, but makes no claims nor guarantees teacher candidates a passing score. Numerical scores are determined by testing companies such as NES or ETS and then compared with individual state standards. A passing score varies from state to state.

Printed in the United States of America

GACE English to Speakers of Other Languages (ESOL)
ISBN: 978-1-60787-063-0

About XAMonline

Founded in 1996, XAMonline began with one teacher in- training who was frustrated by the lack of materials available for certification exam preparation. From a single state-specific guide, XAMonline has grown to offer guides for every state exam, as well as the PRAXIS series.

Each study guide offers more than just the competencies and skills required to pass the test. The core text material leads the teacher beyond rote memorization of skills to mastery of subject matter, a necessary step for effective teaching.

XAMonline's unique publishing model brings currency and innovation to teacher preparation.

- Print on demand technology allows for the most up-to-date guides that are first to market when tests change or are updated.
- The highest quality standards are maintained by using seasoned, professional teachers who are experts in their fields to author the guides.
- Each guide includes varied levels of rigor in a comprehensive practice test so that the study experience closely matches the actual in-test experience.
- The content of the guides is relevant and engaging.

At its inception, XAMonline was a forward-thinking company, and we remain committed to bring new ways of studying and learning to the teaching profession. We choose from a pool of over 1500 certified teachers to review, edit, and write our guides. We partner with technology firms to bring innovation to study habits, offering online test functionality, a personalized flash card builder, and ebooks that allow teachers in training to make personal notes, highlight, and study the material in a variety of ways.

To date, XAMonline has helped nearly 500,000 teachers pass their certification or licensing exams. Our commitment to preparation exceeds the expectation of simply providing the proper material for study; it extends from helping teachers gain mastery of the subject matter and giving them the tools to become effective classroom leaders to ushering today's students towards a successful future.

How to Use This Book

Help! Where do I begin?

Begin at the beginning. Our informal polls show that most people begin studying up to eight weeks prior to the test date. Start early. Then ask yourself some questions: How much do you really know? Are you coming to the test fresh from your teacher education program or do you have to review subjects you haven't considered in ten years? Either way, take a diagnostic or assessment test first. Spend time on sample tests so that you become accustomed to the way the actual test will appear.

A diagnostic can help you decide how to manage your study time, as well as reveal things about your knowledge. Although this guide is structured to follow the order of the test, you are not required to study in that order. By finding a time management and study plan that fits your life, you will be more effective. The results of your diagnostic or self-assessment test can to manage your time and point you toward areas that need more attention.

You may also want to structure your study time based on the percentage of questions on the test. For example, 25% of the mathematics questions focus on algebraic concepts.* **Note,** this doesn't mean that algebraic concepts are equal to 25% of the test's worth. Remember the distribution charts from above: each major content area is devoted an equal amount of questions, but within the content areas the number of questions per subject area varies greatly. Depending on your grasp of any one topic, you may want to devote time comparable to the number of questions. See the example study rubric below for an idea of how you might structure your study plan.

Week	Activity
8 weeks prior to test	Take a diagnostic or pre-assessment test, then build your study plan according to your time availability and areas that need the most work.
7 weeks prior to test	Read the entire study guide. This does not have to be an in-depth reading, but you should take the time to mark sections or areas you'd like to return to that can be skimmed in further study.
6-3 weeks prior to test	For each of these 4 weeks, choose a content area to study. You don't have to go in the order of the book. You may start with the content that needs the most review. Alternatively, you may want to ease yourself into your plan by starting with the most familiar material.
2 weeks prior to test	Take the sample test, score it, and create a review plan for the final week before the test.

1 week prior to test	Go back and study the sections that align with questions you got wrong. Then go back and study the sections related to the questions you answered correctly. If need be, create flashcards and drill yourself on any area that makes you anxious.

Other Helpful Study and Testing Tips

How you study is as important as **what** you study. You can increase your chances of mastering the information by taking some simple, effective steps.

Study Tips

1. You are what you eat. Certain foods aid the learning process by releasing natural memory enhancers called CCKs (cholecystokinin) composed of tryptophan, choline, and phenylalanine. All of these chemicals enhance the neurotransmitters associated with memory. A light meal or snacks from the following foods may help with recall:

   - Milk
   - Nuts and seeds
   - Rice
   - Oats
   - Eggs
   - Turkey
   - Fish

The better the connections, the more you comprehend!

2. The pen is mightier than the sword. Learn to take great notes. In our modern culture, we have grown accustomed to getting our information in small doses. We've subconsciously trained ourselves to assimilate information in neat little packages. Messy notes fragment the flow of information. Your notes can be much clearer with proper formatting. The Cornell method is one such format. This method was popularized in *How to Study in College,* Ninth Edition, by Walter Pauk. You can benefit from the method without purchasing an additional book by simply looking up the method on line. On the next page is a sample of how the Cornell *m*ethod can be adapted for use with this guide.

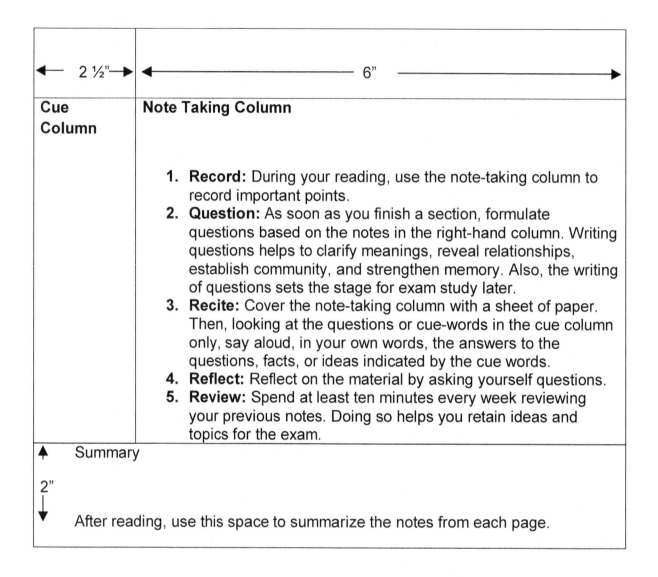

2 ½" 6"

Cue Column

Note Taking Column

1. **Record:** During your reading, use the note-taking column to record important points.
2. **Question:** As soon as you finish a section, formulate questions based on the notes in the right-hand column. Writing questions helps to clarify meanings, reveal relationships, establish community, and strengthen memory. Also, the writing of questions sets the stage for exam study later.
3. **Recite:** Cover the note-taking column with a sheet of paper. Then, looking at the questions or cue-words in the cue column only, say aloud, in your own words, the answers to the questions, facts, or ideas indicated by the cue words.
4. **Reflect:** Reflect on the material by asking yourself questions.
5. **Review:** Spend at least ten minutes every week reviewing your previous notes. Doing so helps you retain ideas and topics for the exam.

Summary

2"

After reading, use this space to summarize the notes from each page.

*Adapted from *How to Study in College,* Ninth Edition, by Walter Pauk, ©Wadsworth, 2008.

3. See the forest for the trees. Get the concept before you look at the details. One way to do this is to take notes as you read, paraphrasing or summarizing in your own words. Putting the concept in terms that are comfortable and familiar may increase retention.

4. Question authority. Ask why, why, why. Pull apart written material paragraph by paragraph and don't forget the captions under the illustrations. For example, if a heading reads *Stream Erosion,* put it in the form of a question ("Why do streams erode?" or "What is stream erosion?") Then find the answer within the material. If you train your mind to think in this manner you will learn more and prepare yourself for answering test questions.

5. Play mind games. Using your brain for reading or puzzles keeps it flexible. Even with a limited amount of time your brain can take in data (much like a computer) and store it for later use. In ten minutes you can: read two paragraphs (at least), quiz yourself with flash cards, or review notes. Even if you don't fully understand something on the first pass, your mind stores it for recall, which is why frequent reading or review increases chances of retention and comprehension.

6. Place yourself in exile and set the mood. Set aside a particular place and time to study that best suits your personal needs and biorhythms. If you're a night person, burn the midnight oil. If you're a morning person set yourself up with some coffee and get to it. Make your study time and place as free from distraction as possible and surround yourself with what you need, be it silence or music. Studies have shown that music can aid in concentration, absorption, and retrieval of information - not all music, though. Classical music is said to work best.

7. Get pointed in the right direction. Use arrows to point to important passages or pieces of information. Arrows are easier to read than a page full of yellow highlights. Highlighting can be used sparingly, but add an arrow to the margin to call attention to it.

8. Check your time budget. You should at least review all the content material before your test, but allocate the most time to the areas that need the most refreshing. It sounds obvious, but it's easy to forget. You can use the study rubric above to balance your study budget.

The proctor will write the start time where it can be seen and later, make you aware of the time remaining, typically 15 minutes before the end of the test.

And Another Thing

Question Types

You're probably thinking, enough already, I want to study! Indulge us a little longer while we explain that there is actually more than one type of multiple-choice question. You can thank us later after you realize how well prepared you are for your exam.

1. **Complete the Statement.** The name says it all. In this question type you'll be asked to choose the correct completion of a given statement. For example: "The Dolch Basic Sight Words consist of a relatively short list of words that children should be able to:

   a. sound out.
   b. know the meaning of.
   c. recognize on sight.
   d. use in a sentence.

   The correct answer is A. In order to check your answer, test out the statement by adding each of the choices to the end of it.

2. **Which of the Following…** One way to test your answer choice for this type of question is to replace the phrase "which of the following" with your selection. Use this example: Which of the following words is one of the twelve most frequently used in children's reading texts?

   a. There
   b. This
   c. The
   d. An

   Don't look! Test your answer. _____ is one of the twelve words most frequently used in children's reading texts. Did you guess C? Then you guessed correctly.

3. **Roman Numeral Choices.** This question type is used when there is more than one possible correct answer. For example: Which of the following two arguments accurately supports the use of cooperative learning as an effective method of instruction?

    I.   Cooperative learning groups facilitate healthy competition between individuals in the group.

    II.   Cooperative learning groups allow academic achievers to carry or cover for academic underachievers.

    III.   Cooperative learning groups make each student in the group accountable for the success of the group.

    IV.   Cooperative learning groups make it possible for students to reward other group members for achieving.

        A. I and II
        B. II and III
        C. I and III
        D. III and IV

Notice that the question states there are **two** possible answers. It's best to read all the possibilities before looking at the answer choices. In this case, the correct answer is D.

4. **Negative Questions.** This type of question contains words such as "not," "least," and "except." Each correct answer will be the statement that does **not** fit the situation described in the question. Such as: Multicultural education is **not**

    a. an idea or concept.
    b. a "tack-on" to the school curriculum.
    c. an educational reform movement.
    d. a process.

Think to yourself that the statement could be anything but the correct answer. This question form is more open to interpretation than other types, so read carefully and don't forget that you're answering a negative statement.

5. Questions That Include Graphs, Tables, or Reading Passages. As ever, read the question carefully. It likely asks for a very specific answer and not broad interpretation of the visual. Here is a simple (though not statistically accurate) example of a graph question: In the following graph, in how many years did more men than women take the PRAXIS II exam?

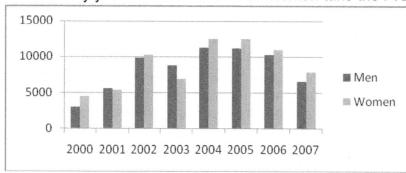

a. None

b. One

c. Two

d. Three

It may help you to simply circle the years that answer the question. Make sure you've read the question thoroughly and once you've made your determination, double check your work. The correct answer is C.

Testing Tips

1. Get smart; play dumb. Sometimes a question is just a question. No one is out to trick you, so don't assume that the test writer is looking for something other than what was asked. Stick to the question as written and don't overanalyze.

2. Do a double take. Read test questions and answer choices at least twice because it's easy to miss something, to transpose a word or some letters. If you have no idea what the correct answer is, skip it and come back later if there's time. If you're still clueless, it's okay to guess. Remember, you're scored on the number of questions you answer correctly and you're not penalized for wrong answers. The worst case scenario is that you miss a point from a good guess.

3. Turn it on its ear. The syntax of a question can often provide a clue, so make things interesting and turn the question into a statement to see if it changes the meaning or relates better (or worse) to the answer choices. {an example would be good here.}

4. Get out your magnifying glass. Look for hidden clues in the questions because it's difficult to write a multiple-choice question without giving away part of the answer in the options presented. In most questions you can readily eliminate one or two potential answers, increasing your chances of answering correctly to 50/50, which will help out if you've skipped a question and gone back to it (see tip #2).

5. Call it intuition. Often your first instinct is correct. If you've been studying the content you've likely absorbed something and have subconsciously retained the knowledge. On questions you're not sure about, trust your instincts because a first impression is usually correct.

6. Graffiti. Sometimes it's a good idea to mark your answers directly on the test booklet and go back to fill in the optical scan sheet later. You don't get extra points for perfectly blackened ovals. If you choose to manage your test in this way, be aware of the risks.Be sure not to mismark your answers when you transcribe to the scan sheet.

7. Become a clock-watcher. You have a set amount of time to answer the questions. Don't get bogged down laboring over a question you're not sure about when there are ten others you could answer more readily. If you choose to follow the advice of tip #6, be sure you leave time near the end to go back and fill in the scan sheet.

Ready? Ready.

Do the Drill

No matter how prepared you feel, it's sometimes a good idea to apply Murphy's Law. The following tips might seem silly, mundane, or obvious, but we're including them anyway.

1. Remember, you are what you eat, so bring a snack. Choose from the list of energizing foods that appear earlier in the introduction.

2. You're not too sexy for your test. Wear comfortable clothes. You'll be distracted if your belt is too tight, or if you're too cold or too hot.

3. Lie to yourself. Even if you think you're a prompt person, pretend you're not and leave plenty of time to get to the testing center. Map it out ahead of time and do a dry run if you have to. There's no need to add road rage to your list of anxieties.

4. Bring **sharp number 2 pencils.** It may seem impossible to forget this need from your school days, but you might. And make sure the erasers are intact, too.

5. No ticket, no test. Bring your admission ticket as well as **two** forms of identification, including one with a picture and signature. You will not be admitted to the test without these things.

6. You can't take it with you. Leave any study aids, dictionaries, notebooks, laptops and the like at home. Certain tests **do** allow a scientific or four-function calculator, so check ahead of time if your test does.

7. Prepare for the desert. Any time spent on a bathroom break **cannot** be made up later, so use your judgment on the amount you eat or drink.

8. Quiet, please! Keeping your own time is a good idea, but not with a timepiece that has a loud ticker. If you use a watch, take it off and place it nearby but not so that it distracts you. And **silence your cell phone.**

To the best of our ability, the content you need to know is represented in this book and in the accompanying online resources. The rest is up to you. You can use the study and testing tips or you can follow your own methods. Either way, you can be confident that there aren't any missing pieces of information and there shouldn't be any surprises in the content on the test.

Good luck!

TEACHER CERTIFICATION STUDY GUIDE

Table of Contents

THIS PAGE BLANK

SUBAREA 1.0   LANGUAGE AND LANGUAGE ACQUISITION

OBJECTIVE 1   **Understand the nature of language and language varieties and ways to apply knowledge of these concepts in the classroom**

SKILL 1.1   **Demonstrate knowledge of the systematic and symbolic nature of language, unique properties of human language (e.g., cultural transmission, displacement, productivity), and concepts related to innateness and universality**

Language is considered by many to be a uniquely human event. The basic units of a language are organized through a complex set of rules. Other characteristics of languages are symbolism, ambiguity, open-endedness (creativity, productivity), ability to be used to discuss other languages (metalanguage) and their use to refer to abstract ideas.
Human beings depend on language to organize and control community life. It is through language that culture is transmitted. Thus, language can be 'displaced', that is, used to discuss events which took place in different places and times (displacement of situations or events which never occurred).

Language is believed to be innate. Many linguists believe it to be programmed into the genetic makeup of the human brain to emerge as the individual develops. Given that the environment and nervous system are normal, all human beings can learn a language.

Even with all the differences, the similarities of languages indicate that languages are subject to universal generalities or constraints. Some of the constraints concern word order and pronoun systems. Many theorists believe these constraints are genetically imposed; others argue that our general cognitive structure limits our language ability, and others believe that the constraints can be explained by the functions language serves. Since universal tendencies are so widespread, it seems logical to suggest that part of our cognitive function is specifically linguistic (Traugott & Pratt, 1980).

SKILL 1.2   **Demonstrate knowledge of basic aspects of language origins and history (e.g., language families, the linguistic history of English)**

An awareness of the **history of the English Language** gives teachers a deeper understanding of the language and sheds light on the fact that languages are constantly changing to serve the needs of their users.

Historically, English evolved from a combination of languages. English is a Germanic language from the family of Indo-European languages. Other Indo-European languages include Latin, Baltic and Slavic. The history of English can be divided into three general periods during which the language experienced significant change.

Old English: In the 5th century, three Germanic tribes crossed the North Sea and invaded the British Isles: the Angles, the Saxons and the Jutes. The Celtic language that had been used by the inhabitants of Britain was replaced by the Germanic language of the Angles. Old English gradually developed from the dialects of the Saxons, consisting of Anglo-Saxon words as well as words from Scandinavian and Latin. Old English is different from modern English in its spelling, pronunciation, vocabulary and grammar rules.

Middle English: In the 11th century, the Normans invaded Britain, and French became the language of the nobility in England. French words were added to English (chamber, desire) and French rules of plural formation were adopted. In the 14th century, King Henry IV became the king of England. He was the first king whose native language was English since the start of the Norman invasion. Middle English began to develop, and its rules were simpler than those of Old English.

Modern English: Middle English gradually evolved into modern English as the phonological system of the language underwent great change, particularly the pronunciation of vowels. Spelling became standardized with the advent of the printing press. As nations had more contact, words from other languages became part of the language, and the language has continued to evolve. The Modern English Shakespeare used in the 16th and early 17th century differs so significantly from today's English that many people have difficulty understanding it.

In the 19th century, when the sun never set on the English empire, English spread to countries all over the world. In addition to spreading the language to England's many political contacts, the language became modified in each location. New Zealand, Canada, South Africa, Australia, and India all participated in this language exchange. In Asia, Africa, and the Americas, thirty-four countries have English as their official language.

American English: Modern English came to America with the Pilgrims. Soon after arriving, they found their language inadequate to describe their new country. They had new topography (*bluff, clearing, prairie*); new plants and food (*live oak, sweet potato, eggplant, squash*); and new experiences (*backwoodsman, squatter, bobsled, and sleigh*). They also found new names for familiar items (*corn* became *maize*) and named American cities after cities in England (*Bath, Salisbury, Exeter, Cambridge,* and *Yarmouth*).

However, the Spanish had arrived in the 15th century and have contributed more words to American English than any other language. *Barbecue, chocolate, tomato, plaza, stampede,* and *tornado,* among many others, come from Spanish. The French influenced language through explorers and missionaries in the north and Midwest. New Orleans developed a distinctive cuisine, architecture, music, and theater. A unique dialect, Cajun, brought words such as *bayou, gopher,* and *picayune* to the language. Early Dutch settlers in New Amsterdam contributed words such as *waffle, coleslaw, cookie,* and *landscape.* The names of some of New York's boroughs were derived from Dutch names: *Breukelyn, Haarlem,* and *Bronck's).*

Germans were the first non-colonizing immigrants, and since their arrival in the late 17th century, people from all over the world have come to the United States, adding their cultures and languages to the already rich blend. Reasons for coming to the United States have varied, but the introduction of new words to American English has been, and will continue to be, an ongoing process of change.

SKILL 1.3   Recognize the effect of language contact on changes in a language and types, sources, and effects of internal variations (e.g., dialects)

Sociolinguistics is the study of how social conditions influence the use of language. Social factors such as ethnicity, religion, gender, status, age, and education all play a role in how individuals use language. Dialects, or "how language is spoken" differ depending on these and other factors. Sociolinguistics seeks to understand the relationship between language and social elements.

Beyond anyone's control, language is constantly changing. In the words of H. L. Mencken, "A living language is like a man suffering incessantly from small hemorrhages, and what it needs above all else is constant transactions of new blood from other tongues. The day the gates go up, that day it begins to die."

France is a prime example of a country that has tried to keep its language "pure." In spite of tremendous efforts, French has evolved. It has acquired new terms for 20th and 21st century technology and experiences. It has been modified by immigrants who have moved to France. Living languages are simply not static.

The United States has experienced unique, disparate social influences, which accounts for the substantial differences between American and other varieties of English, even British English, from which it originated. Ralph Waldo Emerson said, "The English language is the sea which receives tributaries from every region under heaven." Most obvious of these tributaries has been the continuous flow of immigrants, who have brought their customs and languages to the U.S. Each culture that joins the country contributes new words, and new immigrants continue to change the language today. Along the U.S./Mexico border, some states have tried to pass English-Only legislation because they fear that Spanish will become the dominant language spoken, but they cannot control how people speak.

Wars have also added words to our language. During WWII people began to use words such as *flak, blitz, R and R, black market, pin-up, mushroom cloud,* and *fallout*. During the Korean conflict, *chopper* and *brainwashing* came into use. During the Vietnam era, *napalm, friendly fire, search-and-destroy mission,* and *the domino theory* entered the language. During the Iraq War we have learned *the green zone, al-Queda,* and *weapons of mass destruction*. Wars also give new meanings to old words, such as *embedded*, which in the context of Iraq refers to news reporters who join army units.

Contemporary culture changes language significantly. Advertisers have such great success that brand names come to represent entire categories of products, such as *Kleenex* for tissue; *Xerox* for photo copy; *Hoover* for vacuum cleaner; and *Coke* for cola. People pick up and use phrases from popular TV shows: *Yabadabadoo; like, cool, man; go-go gadget; meathead; and duh!* Other cultural trends, such as the drug culture, sports, and fads add new words to the language.

Political rhetoric also influences language. We hear sports metaphors (a success referred to as a home run); war metaphors (victories or defeats); and business metaphors (ending up in the red or the black). Politicians like to "send a message" to enemies, political rivals, or the American people. Candidates like to be "the candidate of change" or "the education candidate", and, of course, no candidate is for increasing taxes, even though they always somehow increase.

Technology and science may have changed language more than any other factor in the past century. An estimated 500,000 technical and scientific terms have been added to English. Many of these words affect our daily lives. Fifty years ago, people didn't routinely use computers, cell phones, the Internet, or satellite dishes. They hadn't had an MRI or wondered if kiwis were safe to eat.

Text messaging, particularly among young people, has created a kind of shorthand variation of English: *CUL8R* means "see you later"; *BRB* means "be right back"; and *TTYL* means "talk to you later." ESL teachers might be surprised at how adroit their students are with technological language. Students who make English-speaking friends and want to adapt to American culture will quickly learn this new language.

In areas where more than one language is spoken, words from languages other than English enter conversations to facilitate communication. The mixing of Spanish and English is sometimes called "Spanglish." A person who intersperses one language with another is code-switching, or mixing words, phrases, or idioms from one language with those of another, perhaps when a word is unknown in the other language.

The merging of languages into English has contributed to the inconsistencies and exceptions to rules that make the language so difficult to learn. It has also increased the number of words one must learn to communicate in English. We can only be certain that English will continue to change and language will continue to be vital in new forms.

A **dialect** is a complete system of verbal communication (oral or signed, but not necessarily written) with its own vocabulary, pronunciation, and grammar. Language variations are often associated with specific regions or social groups. Variations of American English may involve pronunciation, sentence structure, vocabulary and expressions. Dialects are influenced by the social context of language usage. Some factors associated with dialectical differences include ethnic background, gender, age, socioeconomic status, and education.

Often people make sweeping generalizations about dialects, categorizing them broadly, such as "a southern drawl" or "a western twang." The term dialect should not be equated with accent alone. Dialects are complex language systems that have a unique set of rules and vocabulary. In the United States there are hundreds of unique dialects. To the trained ear, the speech of Louisiana dialects is significantly different and distinguishable from Texas dialects, for example, even though we might categorize all of these speakers as having a southern drawl. Other dialects show more profound contrast. When comparing the difference between upper-class Boston Brahman speech, which sounds formal and closely related to British English, and Black English, which has a completely different tone and vocabulary, the two sound almost like completely different languages.

Black English provides a good example of a language system that has well-developed, consistent rules. For example, in Black English the third person singular form of verbs drops the "s" that standard English uses, so the standard English, "She wants that toy." becomes "She want that toy." Black English also drops helping verbs and adds words that previously did not exist in English: "You jivin' me."

Any dialect that has established consistent patterns of sounds and grammar is a legitimate language system. It has no more or less validity than any other language. However, in academia we teach what is considered contemporary standard English. Certainly within standard English one experiences variations of pronunciation and grammar rules, but overall there is a reasonably consistent set of rules that can and should be taught to ELLs.

In the ESL classroom it is worthwhile to have ELLs reflect on and discuss dialectical differences in their first language. Recognizing the types of differences that exist among dialects makes learners more aware of how language works. It also may reduce the mystery of why they have much more difficulty understanding some people than others. Language in general is fluid and ever-changing. Change occurs gradually over time, according to how people speak. New words are added, words drop out of use, and even grammar evolves. For example, over the past 50 years, the past participle of "to get" has gradually changed from "gotten" to "got": I have got tired of waiting. Evolutionary language changes tend to simplify or reduce the language. Social and regional influences on language also have significant impact. Dialects emerge to adapt the language to the purpose and identity of the speaker. Teachers having an insight on this sociolinguistic aspect of the language will have a deeper understanding of how the language works and will be better equipped to teach Standard English to ELLs.

SKILL 1.4 Demonstrate knowledge of pragmatic features of oral and written language that influence or convey meaning (e.g., use of formal and informal styles, idiomatic expressions, nonverbal elements)

Pragmatics is the study of how the context impacts the interpretation of language. Situations dictate language choice, body language, degree of intimacy, and how meaning is interpreted. For example, when customers walk into a bar and sit down on a stool, they expect a bartender will ask them several questions: "What would you like to drink?" and "Would you like to start a tab?" This sequence of events and cues is a typical pattern of interaction in a bar. Pragmatic knowledge provides the customer with a set of expectations for the flow of events. Pragmatic knowledge sets customer expectations. Typically people in a bar expect a certain level of social exchange that allows congeniality without intrusiveness. They expect to receive a certain level of service, and to use a particular level of manners. These types of exchanges are fairly universal in bars, but would be completely inappropriate in a more formal setting, for example, such as conversing with the president of a corporation.

Gestures, the appropriate distance between speakers, seating arrangements, nodding or shaking of the head, signs, and touch are all examples of nonverbal pragmatic conventions. These elements are different in different cultures and can be taught.

In the ESL classroom, pragmatics can be illustrated and practiced by repeating the same situation in different contexts. For example, students can write or act out how they would explain to three different people why they failed a test: their best friend, their teacher, and their parent. With a little imagination, different scenarios can be chosen that pique student interest and make learning fun. For example, explain an embarrassing event in different contexts, such as in front of a boy/girl you want to impress, a close friend, and an authority figure. For students with very low language skills, pantomime can encourage participation, teach the concept, and set up an opportunity for using language to describe what has happened.

SKILL 1.5 Demonstrate knowledge of the influence of various factors (e.g., culture, politics, society) on a speaker's choice of pragmatic features and language variations

Comparing the **customs** of various cultures provides another opportunity for illustrating how context affects meaning, especially when students in a class represent a variety of cultures, For example, in other parts of the world, especially parts of Europe and the Middle East, people commonly greet each other by kissing on both cheeks, even if meeting for the first time. However, in many countries, including the United States, this greeting is not practiced, and is culturally unacceptable in some contexts. For some people this practice would even be offensive or might be ridiculed. Describing and comparing cultural practices provides language practice and demonstrates meaning in context.

Explaining the nuances of English requires ongoing reinforcement. As examples surface, they should be explained and alternative ways to express the same message explored to clarify or expand on the meaning. Pragmatic features in communication can be very indirect. For example, when parents say to their children, "Have you finished your homework?" they are implying a command that if homework has not been completed, the children should stop their current activity and finish their homework. The pragmatic features are found in what was actually said, as well as what was not said. Students can generate their own questions that have farther-reaching implications. **Politics** also affects the pragmatics of different situations. Many political leaders speak in the first person plural form ('We" ....) when addressing their subjects or electorate to indicate that they are speaking from a position of power or for the greater good. This use of the "royal we" also removes the politician from accepting individual responsibility.

Society imposes many rules that are unconsciously observed by its members. Fox example, English speakers normally read from left to right and therefore, would alphabetize books from left to right on a shelf. However, many languages are read from right to left. Teachers need to be aware of these differences and maintain a rich visual and textual environment in the classroom through pictures and texts. Visitors from different cultures (think of the numerous differences between American, Canadian, English, and Australian cultures, for example) can help by discussing societal differences with the students.

SKILL 1.6 **Identify strategies that apply knowledge of pragmatics to help ELL students respond appropriately and communicate effectively in a variety of contexts, including formal and informal settings, and for a variety of audiences and purposes (e.g., interpreting and responding to nonverbal cues and body language and demonstrating knowledge of acceptable nonverbal classroom behaviors)**

For students from other cultures, pragmatics involving nonverbal cues and body language can be confusing. It is the teacher's responsibility to be sensitive, to acknowledge these different behaviors when they become obvious in the classroom, and to guide students to behaviors appropriate to their audience, purpose, and setting.

Students may be unaware that others feel uncomfortable because they are standing too close or avoiding eye contact, yet these are very common examples of nonverbal communication which are culturally different. In some cultures, it is considered impolite to look a teacher in the eye—exactly the opposite behavior North Americans expect! The problem could be addressed directly by discussing appropriate behaviors in different cultures, perhaps by focusing on behavior appropriate to the teacher as a model.

Other examples of nonverbal communication are gestures and using acceptable tone, volume, stress, and intonation in different social settings. Voice volume is a learned behavior. All students (not just ELLs) need to learn the appropriate volume for different settings such as the library, hall, gymnasium, supermarket, and movie theater. An appropriate correction for young children would be to ask all the class to use their "inside" voices and not their "outside" (playground) voices when speaking in the classroom.

COMPETENCY 2.0 **Understand the phonology, morphology, syntax, semantics, and discourse of the English language as related to the development of listening, speaking, reading, writing, and viewing for social and academic purposes**

SKILL 2.1 **Demonstrate knowledge of phonology and identify strategies that apply knowledge of phonology to help ELL students develop oral language (e.g., discrimination and pronunciation of English phonemes, intonation), reading, and writing skills including spelling, in English**

The definition of **phonology** can be summarized as "the way in which speech sounds form patterns" (Diaz-Rico, Weed, 1995). Phonology is a subset of the linguistics field, which studies the organization and systems of sound within a particular language. Phonology is based on the theory that every native speaker unconsciously retains the sound structure of that language and is more concerned with the sounds than with the physical process of creating those sounds.

When babies babble or make what we call "baby sounds," they are actually experimenting with all of the sounds represented in all languages. As they learn a specific language, they become more proficient in the sounds of that language and forget how to make sounds that they don't need or use.

Phonemes, pitch, and **stress** are all components of phonology. Because each affects the meaning of communications, they are variables that ELLs must recognize and learn. Phonology analyzes the sound structure of the given language by:

- determining which phonetic sounds have the most significance.
- explaining how these sounds influence a native speaker of the language.

For example, the Russian alphabet has a consonant, which, when pronounced, sounds like the word "rouge" in French. English speakers typically have difficulty pronouncing this sound pattern, because inherently they know this is not a typical English sound-- even though it occasionally is encountered (Díaz-Rico, Weed, 1995).

Mastering a sound that does not occur in the learner's first language requires ongoing repetition, both hearing the sound and attempting to say it. The older the learner, the more difficult this process becomes, especially if the learner has only spoken one language before reaching puberty. Correct pronunciation may literally require years of practice because initially the learner may not hear the sound correctly. Expecting an ELL to master a foreign pronunciation quickly leads to frustration for the teacher and the learner. With enough focused repetition, however, the learner may eventually hear the difference and then be able to imitate it. Inadequate listening and speaking practice will result in a persistent heavy accent.

Phonemes are the smallest units of sound that affect meaning, i.e. distinguish two words. In English, there are approximately 44 speech sounds yet only 26 letters, so the sounds, when combined, become words. For this reason, English is not considered a phonetic language—a language where there is a one-to-one correspondence between letters and sounds. For example, consider the two words, "pin" and "bin." The only difference is the first consonant of the words, the "p" in "pin" and "b" in "bin." This makes the sounds "p" and "b" phonemes in English, because the difference in sound creates a difference in meaning.

Focusing on phonemes to provide pronunciation practice allows students to have fun while they learn to recognize and say sounds. Pairs or groups of words that have a set pattern make learning easier. For example, students can practice saying or thinking of words that rhyme but begin with a different phoneme, such as tan, man, fan, and ran. Other groups of words might start with the same phoneme followed by various vowel sounds, such as ten, ton, tan, and tin. This kind of alliteration can be expanded into tongue twisters that students find challenging and fun.

Vowels and consonants should be introduced in a deliberate order to allow combinations that form real words, though "made-up" words that have no real meaning in English may also be encouraged when introducing new sounds.

Pitch in communication determines the context or meaning of words or series of words. A string of words can communicate more than one meaning, for example, when posed as a question or statement. For example, the phrase "I can't go" acts as a statement, if the pitch or intonation falls. However, the same phrase becomes the question "I can't go?" if the pitch or intonation rises for the word "go."

Stress can occur at a "word" or "sentence" level. At the "word" level, different stresses on the syllable can actually modify the word's meaning. Consider the word "conflict." To pronounce it as a noun, one would stress the first syllable, as in "cónflict." However, to use it as a verb, the second syllable would be stressed, as in "conflíct."

Different dialects sometimes pronounce the same word differently, even though both pronunciations have the same meaning. For example, in some parts of the United States the word "insurance" is pronounced by stressing the second syllable, while in other parts of the country the first syllable is stressed.

At the "sentence" level, stress can also be used to vary the meaning. For example, consider the following questions and how the meaning changes, according to the stressed words:

> **He** did that? (Emphasis in on the person)
> He **did** that? (Emphasis is on the action)
> He did **that**? (Emphasis is on object of the action)

This type of meaning differentiation is difficult for most ELL students to grasp, and requires innovative teaching, such as acting out the three different meanings. However, since pitch and stress can change the meaning of a sentence completely, students must learn to recognize these differences. Not recognizing sarcasm or anger can cause students considerable problems in their academic and everyday endeavors.

Unlike languages such as Spanish or French, English has multiple pronunciations of vowels and consonants which contribute to making it a difficult language to learn. Phonetic rules are critical to learning to read and write, in spite of their numerous exceptions, but they do little to assist listening and speaking skills.

Phonographemics refers to the study of letters and letter combinations. Unlike most languages, in English one symbol can represent many phonemes. While some phonetic rules apply, English has numerous exceptions, which make it difficult to learn.

In teaching English to speakers of other languages, the wide variation of phonemes represented by a single symbol must be taught and *drilled*. If it is difficult for native speakers to learn the English spelling system, it's a great leap for the foreign language learner. Graphemes should be introduced long after spoken English. Students must first begin to be able to speak and hear the language before they can be taught to spell it. The phonology of English is an important component of an ESOL program.

Phonographemic differences between words of English are a common source of confusion and thus need to be taught explicitly with plenty of learning activities to enable learners to acquire them sufficiently. Some areas of focus for the ESOL classroom include

Homonyms: A general term that describes word forms that have two or more meanings, e.g., can (to be able) and can (a container).

Homographs: Two or more words that have the same spelling or pronunciation but different meanings, e.g., stalk (part of a plant) / stalk (follow)

Homophones: Two or more words that have the same pronunciation but different meanings and spelling, e.g., wood/would, cite/sight

Heteronyms: Two or more words that have the same spelling, but have a different pronunciation and meaning, e.g., Polish/polish

Some useful activities for instruction would be to identify misspelled words, to recognize multiple meanings of words and sentences, to spell words correctly within a given context, and to match words with their meanings.

SKILL 2.2   Demonstrate knowledge of morphology and identify strategies that apply knowledge of morphology to promote ELL students' development of vocabulary and literacy skills, including spelling, in English

Morphology refers to the process of how the words of a language are formed to create meaningful messages. ESOL teachers need to be aware of the principles of morphology in English to provide meaningful activities that will help in the process of language acquisition.

Morphemic analysis requires breaking a word down into its component parts to determine its meaning. It shows the relationship between the root or base word and the prefix and/or suffix to determine the word's meaning.

A **morpheme** is the smallest unit of language system which has meaning. These units are more commonly known as: the root word, the prefix, and the suffix. They cannot be broken down into any smaller units.

- **The root word or base word** is the key to understanding a word, because this is where the actual meaning is determined.
- **A prefix** acts as a syllable, which appears in front of the root or base word and can alter the meaning of the root or base word.
- **A suffix** is a letter or letters, which are added to the end of the word and can alter the original tense or meaning of the root or base word.

The following is an example of how morphemic analysis can be applied to a word:

- Choose a root or base word, such as "kind."
- Create as many new words as possible, by changing the prefix and suffix.
- New words, would include unkind, kindness, mankind, and kindly.

Learning common roots, prefixes, and suffixes greatly helps ELLs to decode unfamiliar words. This can make a big difference in how well a student understands written language. Students who can decode unfamiliar words become less frustrated when reading in English and, as a result, are likely to read more. They have greater comprehension and their language skills improve more quickly. Having the tools to decode unfamiliar words enables ELL students to perform better on standardized tests because they are more likely to understand the question and answer choices.

Guessing at the meaning of words should be encouraged. Too often students become dependent on translation dictionaries, which impede the development of morphemic analysis skills. Practice should include identifying roots, prefixes, and suffixes, as well as using morphemic knowledge to form new words.

ESOL learners need to understand the structure of words in English, and how words may be created and altered. Some underlying principles of the morphology of English are:

1. Morphemes may be free and able to stand by themselves (e.g., chair, bag) or they may be bound or derivational, needing other morphemes to create meaning (e.g., read-able, en-able).
2. Knowledge of the meanings of derivational morphemes such as prefixes and suffixes enables students to decode word meanings and create words in the language through word analysis, e.g., un-happy means not happy.
3. Some morphemes in English provide grammatical rather than semantic information to words and sentences (e.g., of, the, and).
4. Words can be combined in English to create new compound words (e.g., key + chain = keychain).

ESOL teachers also need to be aware that principles of morphology from the native language may be transferred to either promote or interfere with the second language learning process.

When students over-generalize a learned rule or simply make a mistake, corrections should be made in a way that does not embarrass the student. Teachers must also consider a student's stage of progress and the context of the error. Correcting every single error is unnecessary when students are experimenting with language and bravely trying to use a language they are struggling to learn. A useful technique is to repeat segments of spoken language, as if to confirm understanding, and correct any errors. This saves face for the student and allows the teacher to demonstrate the correct word use or pronunciation. If the student fails to notice the correction and makes the same error again, the teacher can repeat the same type of correction. Teachers can also demonstrate variations of words in this manner, such as using a different verb tense to paraphrase what was said.

Correcting every error in a writing sample can discourage participation and cause students to shut down to learning. Keeping track of errors that students repeat allows the teacher to re-teach specific skills or address specific needs, either with a group of students who all need to master that skill, or individually for a student who has not yet mastered a skill after others in the class.

SKILL 2.3 Demonstrate knowledge of syntax and identify strategies that apply knowledge of syntax to promote ELL students' social and academic language and literacy development in English

Syntax involves the order in which words are arranged to create meaning. Different languages use different patterns for sentence structure. Syntax also refers to the rules for creating correct sentence patterns. English, like many other languages, is a subject-verb-object language, which means that in most sentences the subject precedes the verb, and the object follows the verb. ELLs whose native language follows a subject-verb-object pattern will find it easier to master English syntax.

The process of second language acquisition includes forming generalizations about the new language and internalizing the rules that are observed. During the silent period, before learners are willing to attempt verbal communication, they are engaged in the process of building a set of syntactic rules for creating grammatically correct sentences in the second language. We don't yet fully understand the nature of this process, but we do know that learners must go through this process of observing, drawing conclusions about language constructs, and testing the validity of their conclusions. This is why learners benefit more from intense language immersion than from corrections.

Language acquisition is a gradual, hierarchical, and cumulative process. This means that learners must go through and master each stage in sequence, much as Piaget theorized for learning in general. In terms of syntax, this means learners must acquire specific grammatical structures, first recognizing the difference between subject and predicate; putting subject before predicate; and learning more complex variations, such as questions, negatives, and relative clauses.

While all learners must pass through each stage and accumulate the language skills learned in each, learners use different approaches to mastering these skills. Some use more cognitive processing procedures, which means their learning takes place more through thought processes. Other learners tend to use psycholinguistic procedures, which employ speech practice as principle means of learning. Regardless of how learners process information, they must all proceed through the same stages, from least to most complicated.

Experts disagree on the exact definition of the phases, but a set of six general stages would include:

Stage of Development	Examples
1. Single words	I; throw; ball
2. SVO structure	I throw the ball.
3. Wh-fronting	Where you are?
Do fronting	Do you like me?
Adverb fronting	Today I go to school.
Negative + verb	She is not nice.
4. Y/N inversion	Do you know him? Yes, I know him.
Copula (linking v) inversion	Is he at school?
Particle shift	Take your hat off.
5. Do 2nd	Why did she leave?
Aux 2nd	Where has he gone?
Neg do 2nd	She does not live here.
6. Cancel inversion	I asked what she was doing.

Each progressive step requires the learner to use knowledge from the previous step, as well as new knowledge of the language. As ELLs progress to more advanced stages of syntax, they may react differently, depending on their ability to acquire the new knowledge needed for mastery. A learner who successfully integrates the new knowledge is a "standardizer"; he/she makes generalizations, eliminates erroneous conclusions, and increasingly uses syntactical rules correctly. However, for some learners, the next step may be more difficult than the learner can manage. These learners become "simplifiers"; they revert to syntactical rules learned at easier stages and fail to integrate the new knowledge. When patterns of errors reflect lower level stages, the teacher must re-teach the new syntactical stage. If simplifiers are allowed to repeatedly use incorrect syntax, they risk having their language become fossilized, which makes learning correct syntax that much more difficult.

SKILL 2.4 Demonstrate knowledge of semantics and identify strategies that apply knowledge of semantics to help ELL students acquire and productively use a wide range of vocabulary in English

Semantics encompasses the meaning of individual words, as well as combinations of words. Native speakers have used their language to function in their daily lives at all levels. Through experience they know the effects of intonation, connotation, and synonyms. This is not true of foreign speakers. In an ESOL class, we are trying to teach as quickly as possible what the native speaker already knows. The objectives of beginning ESOL lesson plans should deliberately build a foundation that will enable students to meet more advanced objectives.

Teaching within a specific context helps students to understand the meaning of words and sentences. When students can remember the context in which they learn words and recall how the words were used, they retain that knowledge and can compare it when different applications of the same words are introduced.

Using words in a variety of contexts helps students reach deeper understanding of the words. They can then guess at new meanings that are introduced in different contexts. For example, the word "conduct" can be taught in the context of conducting a meeting or an investigation. Later the word "conductor" can be used in various contexts that demonstrate some similarity but have distinctly different uses, such as a conductor of electricity, the conductor of a train, or the conductor of an orchestra.

Second language learners must learn to translate words and sentences that they already understand in their primary language into the language they wish to acquire. This can be a daunting task because of the many ways meaning is created in English. Voice inflection, variations of meaning, variations of usage, and emphasis are among the factors that affect meaning. The lexicon of language includes the stored meaning, contextual meaning from word association, knowledge of pronunciation and grammar, and morphemes.

Idioms, particularly those that cannot be translated literally, present a particular challenge to ELLs. Here again, creating contexts facilitates learning. Grouping idioms according to types of language use helps. Some idioms rely on synonyms, some hyperbole, others metaphor. Having students translate idioms from their native language into English strengthens their ability to appreciate the meaning of idioms. Also, creating their own original idioms increases understanding.

How idioms are taught greatly affects how well they are remembered and the level of frustration the ELL experiences. Visual representations of idioms make meaning easier to understand and provide a memory cue to prompt recall. Using commercially produced illustrations or drawing their own representations of the meaning makes learning idioms easier and more fun. Students can also write stories or perform skits that illustrate the meaning of idioms.

SKILL 2.5 **Demonstrate knowledge of discourse (e.g., analyzing oral and written discourse with respect to cohesion and coherence, identifying similarities and differences between language structures used in spoken and written English, analyzing text structures, recognizing turn-taking practices); and identify strategies that apply knowledge of discourse to help ELL students understand a variety of texts and genres and engage in oral and written discourse that is fluent, cohesive, and coherent**

The term **discourse** refers to linguistic units composed of several sentences and is derived from the concept of "discursive formation" or communication that involves specialized knowledge of various kinds. Discourse plays a role in all spoken and written language. Discourse shapes the way language is transmitted and how we organize our thoughts. Conversations, arguments, or speeches are types of **spoken discourse**.

The structure of discourse varies among languages and traditions. For example, Japanese writing does not present the main idea at the beginning of an essay; rather, writing builds up to the main idea, which is presented or implied at the end of the essay. This is completely different than English writing, which typically presents the main idea or thesis at the beginning of an essay and repeats it at the end.

In addition to language and structure, topic or focus affects discourse. The discourse in various disciplines (such as feminist studies, cultural studies, and literary theory) approaches topics differently.

Discourse between speakers of English requires knowledge of certain protocols in addition to other aspects of language. Speakers should have the necessary skills to maintain the momentum of a conversation, as well as to correct misunderstandings. Typical spoken discourse follows predictable patterns. For example, one person might say, "I saw a good movie last night." The other person would ask, "What was it about?" The first person then answers in a paragraph with a topic sentence: "It was about a bunch of guys who devised a plan to rob a casino," and then proceeds to fill in the details.

Vocal discourse varies significantly depending on context. People speak in different registers depending on to whom they are talking and what the occasion calls for. A candidate who is running for president and speaking to a group will use more formal speech than in a casual conversation. The message conveyed may also vary, depending on whether the group is one of supporters or people who hold different political views. In either case, the candidate must make choices about how to organize what he/she says to ensure comprehension and to hold the audience's interest.

ELLs might initially practice set conversations to learn the patterns of English discourse. Practicing in pairs using a question and answer format gives both participants an opportunity to learn the structures of discourse as well as information about the other person or the other person's culture. Such practice also gives students practice with other language skills and can increase vocabulary. The teacher may provide a set of questions and learners can alternate asking and answering. Short skits that repeat a limited number of words also provide helpful practice. Allowing students time to converse informally, perhaps using suggested topics, continues to reinforce speech patterns.

Polite discourse includes what is called "empty language" or perfunctory speech that has little meaning but is important in social exchanges. Frequently English speakers start a conversation by asking, "How are you?" even though they have no real interest in the other person's health. An appropriate response would be, "Fine." even if the person may not feel well. The exchange is simply a polite means of starting a conversation. Likewise, at the end of a discourse empty language is frequently employed: "It was good to see you." "Good to see you, too." This type of discourse is part of Basic Interpersonal Communication Skills (**BICS**), which learners must acquire to function in social situations. It is generally less demanding than Cognitive Academic Language Proficiency (**CALP**), and allows learners to participate in informal discourses.

Written discourse ranges from the most basic grouping of sentences to the most complicated essays and stories. Regardless of the level, English writing demands certain structure patterns. A typical paragraph begins with a topic sentence, which states directly or indirectly the focus of the paragraph, adds supporting ideas and details, and ends with a concluding sentence that relates to the focus and either states the final thought on that topic or provides a transition to the next paragraph. As with spoken discourse, organization, tone, and word choice are critical to transferring thoughts successfully and maintaining interest.

As skills increase, paragraphs are combined into stories or essays. Each type of writing has specific components and structures. Story writing requires setting, plot, and character. Initially, following a chronological order is probably easiest for ELLs, but as learners become more skillful, other types of order should be practiced, such as adding descriptions in spatial order.

Teachers frequently rely on the proverbial three- or five-paragraph essay to teach essay writing because it provides a rigid structure for organizing and expanding ideas within a single focus. It mirrors the paragraph structure organizationally in that the first, introductory paragraph provides the main idea or focus of the essay; each body paragraph adds and develops a supporting idea and details; and the concluding paragraph provides a summary or other type of conclusion that relates to the main idea or focus stated in the first paragraph. Obviously, no one considers such mechanical essays to be the ultimate goal of essay writing. However, especially for ELLs, having a rigid structure teaches the basic organizational concept of English essays. By offering strictly defined limits, the teacher reduces the number of variables to learn about essay writing. Starting with a blank page can be overwhelming to ELLs. Working within this structure enables learners to focus on developing each paragraph, a challenging enough task when one considers the language skills required! As learners become better able to control their writing and sustain a focus, variations can be introduced and topics expanded.

Language proficiency requires both BICS and CALP. While these categories have clear distinctions, they also have underlying similarities that contribute to overall language learning. Students should also recognize Common Underlying Proficiency (**CUP**). This category is made up of skills, ideas, and concepts that learners can transfer from their first language to their English learning. Both similarities and differences between languages can help learners comprehend and learn aspects of English.

SKILL 2.6   Recognize the importance of serving as a good language model for ELL students and for providing opportunities for ELL students to be exposed to a variety of proficient English speakers

ELL students need to be exposed to authentic, natural English in the classroom setting as well as in settings outside the classroom. To achieve this goal, the ESOL teacher should be a good language model, first of all. Foreigners frequently complain that English speakers swallow their words or have mashed potatoes in their mouths. The teacher needs to be aware of this potential problem and speak slowly and distinctly, especially when communicating new information. This will help the ELLs become acquainted with the rhythm patterns of English.

However, teachers should not be afraid to expose students to nonnative speakers of English. Today, the number of nonnative speakers of English is far greater than the number of native English speakers! Opportunities to hear a variety of speakers may be accomplished by additional listening exercises using taped stories and music, CDs, videos, field trips, and classroom visitors. These opportunities may all be necessary to help students obtain a wide range of experiences to maintain high motivation and promote language learning.

COMPETENCY 3.0   Understand first and second language acquisition

SKILL 3.1   Demonstrate knowledge of current theories and research in first and second language acquisition

Between two and three years of age, most children will be able to use language to influence the people closest to them. Research shows that, in general, boys acquire language more slowly than girls, which means we need to consider very carefully how we involve boys in activities designed to promote early language and literacy. Various theories have tried to explain the **language acquisition process**, including:

Chomsky: Language Acquisition Device

Chomsky's theory, described as Nativist, asserts that humans are born with a special biological brain mechanism, called a Language Acquisition Device (LAD). His theory supposes that the ability to learn language is innate, that nature is more important than nurture, and that experience using language is only necessary in order to activate the LAD. Chomsky based his assumptions on work in linguistics. His work shows that children's language development is much more complex than Behaviorist Theory, which believes that children learn language merely by being rewarded for imitating. However, Chomsky's theory underestimates the influence that thought (cognition) and language have on each other's development.

Piaget: Cognitive Constructivism

Piaget's central interest was children's cognitive development. He theorized that language is simply one way that children represent their familiar worlds, a reflection of thought, and that language does not contribute to the development of thinking. He believed cognitive development precedes language development.

Vygotsky: Social Constructivism and Language

Unlike Chomsky and Piaget, Vygotsky's central focus is the relationship between the development of thought and language. He was interested in the ways different languages impact a person's thinking. He suggests that what Piaget saw as young children's egocentric speech was actually private speech, the child's way of using words to think about something, which progressed from social speech to thinking in words. Vygotsky views language first as social communication, which gradually promotes both language itself and cognition.

Recent theorizing: Intentionality
Some contemporary researchers and theorists criticize earlier theories and suggest children, their behaviors, and their attempts to understand and communicate are misunderstood when the causes of language development are thought to be 'outside' the child or else mechanistically 'in the child's brain.' They recognize that children are active learners who co-construct their worlds. Their language development is part of their holistic development, emerging from cognitive, emotional, and social interactions. They believe language development depends on the child's social and cultural environment, the people in it, and their interactions. How children represent these factors in their minds is fundamental to language development. They believe a child's agenda and the interactions generated by the child promote language learning. The adult's role, actions, and speech are still considered important, but adults need to be able to "mind read" and adjust their side of the co-construction to relate to an individual child's understanding and interpretation.

Theories about language development help us see that enjoying 'proto-conversations' with babies (treating them as people who understand, share and have intentions in sensitive interchanges), and truly listening to young children, are the best ways to promote their language development.

Brain research has shown that the single most important factor affecting **language acquisition** is the onset of puberty. Before puberty, a person uses one area of the brain for language learning; after puberty, a different area of the brain is used. A person who learns a second language before reaching puberty will always process language learning as if pre-pubescent. A person who begins to learn a second language after the onset of puberty will likely find language learning more difficult and depend more on repetition.

Some researchers have focused on analyzing aspects of the language to be acquired. Factors they consider include:

- Error analysis: recognizing patterns of errors
- Interlanguage: analyzing what aspects of the target language are universal
- Developmental Patterns: the order in which features of a language are acquired and the sequence in which a specific feature is acquired

SKILL 3.2   Demonstrate knowledge of processes and stages of first and second language acquisition and literacy development

Stephen Krashen developed a **theory of second language acquisition**, which helps explain the **processes used** by adults when learning a second language:

The Acquisition-Learning hypothesis: There is a difference between "learning" a language and "acquiring" it. Children "acquire" a first language using the same process they used to learn their first language. However, adults who know only one language have to "learn" a language through coursework, studying, and memorizing. One can acquire a second language, but often it requires more deliberate interaction within that language.

The Monitor Hypothesis: The learned language "monitors" the acquired language. In other words, this is when a person's "grammar check" kicks in and keeps awkward, incorrect language out of a person's L2 communication.

The Natural Order Hypothesis: The learning of grammatical structures is predictable and follows a "natural order."

The Input Hypothesis: A language learner will learn best when the instruction or conversation is just above the learner's ability. That way, the learner has the foundation to understand most of the language but will have to figure out, often in context, the unknown elements. Some people call this "comprehensible input."

The Affective Filter Hypothesis: People will learn a second language when they are relaxed, have high levels of motivation, and have a decent level of self-confidence.

Teaching students who are learning English as a second language poses some unique challenges, particularly in a standards-based environment. Teachers should teach with the student's developmental level in mind. Instruction should not be "dummied-down" for ESOL students. Different approaches should be used to ensure that these students get multiple opportunities to learn and practice English and still learn content.

L1 (acquired language) and L2 (learned language) learning follow many, if not all, of the same steps.

- **Silent Period:** The stage when a learner knows perhaps 500 receptive words but feels uncomfortable producing speech. The absence of speech does not indicate a lack of learning, and teachers should not try to force the learner to speak. Comprehension can be checked by having the learner point or mime in response to instructions.. Also known as the Receptive or Preproduction stage.

- **Private Speech:** When the learner knows about 1,000 receptive words and speaks in one- or two-word phrases. The learner can use simple responses, such as yes/no, either/or. Also known as the Early Production stage.

- **Lexical Chunks:** The learner knows about 3,000 receptive words and can communicate using short phrases and sentences. Long sentences typically have grammatical errors. Also known as the Speech Emergence stage.

- **Formulaic Speech:** The learner knows about 6,000 receptive words and begins to make complex statements, state opinions, ask for clarification, share thoughts, and speak at greater length. Also known as the Intermediate Language Proficiency stage.
- **Experimental or Simplified Speech:** When the learner develops a level of fluency and can make semantic and grammar generalizations. Also known as the Advanced Language Proficiency stage.

Researchers disagree on whether the development of Formulaic Speech and Experimental or Simplified Speech is the same for L1 and L2 learners. Regardless, understanding that students must go through a predictable, sequential series of stages helps teachers to recognize the student's progress and respond effectively. Providing comprehensible input will help students advance their language learning at any stage.

SKILL 3.3   Examine the role of the primary language (L1) in acquiring English as a second language (L2), including the process of transferring language and reading skills from L1 to L2, and demonstrate knowledge of strategies for building on ELL students' current language skills as a foundation for learning English

Language, barring physical disabilities or isolation from other humans, is universal. Developing language is a lifelong process in one's native language and similar processes must be gone through to thoroughly acquire or learn a foreign language. Many studies have found that cognitive and academic development in the **first language** has an extremely important and positive effect on second language schooling (e.g. Bialystok, 1991; Collier, 1989, 1992; Garcia, 1994; Genesee, 1987, 1994; Thomas & Collier, 1995). It is, therefore, important that language learners continue to develop their first language skills because the most gifted five-year-old is approximately half way through the process of first language development. From the ages of 6 to 12, the child continues to acquire subtle phonological distinctions, vocabulary, semantics, syntax, formal discourse patterns, and the complexities of pragmatics in the oral system of their first language (Berko & Gleason, 1993).

These skills can be transferred to acquiring or learning a second language. When ELLs already know how to read and write in their first language, they can transfer many of their primary language skills to their target language. They have already learned the relationship between print and spoken language, that print can be used for many different things, and that writing conveys messages from its author. Grellet (1981) has stated that the "knowledge one brings to the text is often more important than what one finds in it." Thus, teachers can build on this previous knowledge and address specifics in English as they arise.

Collier emphasizes that students who do not reach a threshold of knowledge in their first language, including literacy, may experience cognitive difficulties in their second language (Collier, 1987; Collier & Thomas, 1989, Cummins, 1981, 1991; Thomas & Collier, 1995). Uninterrupted cognitive development is key. It is a disservice to parents and children to encourage the use of second language instead of first language at home, precisely because both are working at a level below their actual cognitive maturity. While non-native speakers in kindergarten through second or third grade may do well if schooled in English part or all of the day, from fourth grade through high school, students with little or no academic or cognitive development in their first language, do less and less well as they move into the upper grades where academic and cognitive demands are greater (Collier, 1995).

SKILL 3.4 Recognize the nature and role of comprehensible input and output for second-language development and demonstrate knowledge of strategies for providing ELL students with comprehensible input and opportunities for producing comprehensible output

In language learning, input is defined as the language information or data to which the learner has access. Learners receive input from their parents, their community, TV, the teacher, the textbook, readers, audio and video tapes, other students in the classroom, etc. It is generally accepted that **comprehensible input** is key to second language learning. Even so, input alone may not lead to second language acquisition. The kind of input must also be taken into consideration.

Krashen believes humans acquire language in only one way: by understanding messages - - that is, receiving comprehensible input. Krashen defines comprehensible input as $i + 1$ or input which is just beyond the learner's present ability. In this way, the learner can move from what he knows to the next level in the natural order of acquisition.

Other theorists report that frequency of certain items in the target language appear to contribute to output (Dulay and Burt, 1974; Schmidt and Frota, 1986).

Collier's (1995) research suggests that classes in schools that are highly interactive, emphasizing student problem-solving and discovery through thematic experiences across the curriculum are likely to provide the kind of social setting for natural language acquisition to take place simultaneously with academic and cognitive development. She continues, "Collaborative interaction in which meaning is negotiated with peers is central to the language acquisition process, for both oral and written language development."

SKILL 3.5 **Recognize the role of meaningful interaction in the development of communicative competence in a new language and demonstrate knowledge of strategies for providing opportunities for ELL students to communicate in a variety of social and academic settings**

Interpersonal communication involves verbal and nonverbal communication. Verbal communication includes both speaking and writing; nonverbal communication includes gestures and deliberate facial expressions. Interpersonal communication is inescapable; even not communicating sends a message to others. It is a complicated process because of the unknowns between communicators and because language is imprecise by nature. Communication is also contextual, so that the same thing said in one context means something entirely different in another. Teaching communication skills requires modeling by the teacher and practicing by the students.

Specific skills include:

- **Summarizing:** A summary presents a condensed version of the original language without losing the basic meaning. Summarizing reflects understanding and the ability to break down a text or verbal exchange into its most important parts. Practicing summarization can be a useful tool for comprehension checks and a good preparation for taking standardized tests. Presenting a summary as a preview of a conversation or text before the ELL listens to or reads it facilitates understanding and reduces frustration.

- **Paraphrasing:** A paraphrase restates what is written or spoken. Paraphrases tend to be longer than the original text or verbal exchange because they add details as they attempt to explain. To paraphrase requires both comprehension and the ability to reinterpret language in much the same way that translation reproduces meaning from one language to another. For ELLs, paraphrasing increases comprehension and offers excellent vocabulary practice. Teachers or students can paraphrase parts of what is spoken or read to ensure students have understood. Paraphrasing also provides a good means to indicate listening and to affirm the speaker.

- **Listening:** Hearing what is spoken requires a more complicated process than simply hearing sounds. A variety of internal and external factors can affect understanding. ELLs must practice listening skills to avoid shutting down or misunderstanding what is said. Caution must be used to encourage active listening and avoid causing barriers. Once words are spoken, they cannot be retrieved.

- **Questioning:** Questions stimulate thinking and learning. They can be used to stimulate interest in an academic topic and to set goals for learning. Initially questions that require a one- or two-word answer should be used until learners have the skills to respond to open-ended questions. Questions can also be used to check for comprehension and to make subtle corrections. Asking good questions is a skill that requires ongoing practice. How a question is asked can either threaten or encourage the listener. Teachers should take care to model good questioning so that it encourages dialog and does not seem like an interrogation.

- **Initiating:** In a conversation, initiating means declaring one's conversational intent and inviting consent from one's prospective conversation partner. It is a means for engaging others in interpersonal communication. Skillful initiating results in active engagement; without it, potential conversations become awkward silences.

- **Turn-taking:** Conversations progress by managing the flow of information back and forth between partners. By taking turns, or alternating roles of speaker and listener, ELLs develop necessary conversational skills. Without these skills, conversations come to an abrupt halt. ELLs can begin by practicing set conversations and progress to initiating and taking turns talking about topics that interest them. Formal and informal conversations must be practiced to prepare learners for the various situations they will encounter.

SKILL 3.6   **Demonstrate knowledge of cognitive processes involved in synthesizing and internalizing a new language (e.g., memorization, categorization, metacognition) and demonstrate knowledge of strategies for explicitly teaching ELL students effective language learning and self-monitoring strategies to promote their language development**

Cognitive strategies

Cognitive strategies are vital to second language acquisition; their most salient feature is the manipulation of the second language. The following are the most basic strategies: "Practicing", "Receiving and Sending Messages", "Analyzing and Reasoning", and "Creating Structure for Input and Output," which can be remembered by the acronym, "PRAC."

Practicing: The following strategies promote the learner's grasp of the language: practice constant repetition, make attempts to imitate a native speaker's accent, concentrate on sounds, and practice in a realistic setting.

Receiving and Sending Messages: These strategies help the learner quickly locate salient points and then interpret the meaning: skim through information to determine "need to know" vs. "nice to know," use available resources (print and non-print) to interpret messages.

Analyzing and Reasoning: Use general rules to understand the meaning and then work into specifics, and break down unfamiliar expressions into parts.

Creating Structure for Input and Output: Choose a format for taking meaningful notes, practice summarizing long passages, use highlighters as a way to focus on main ideas or important specific details.

Metacognitive Strategies
The ESOL teacher is responsible for helping students become aware of their own individual learning strategies and constantly improve those strategies and add to them. Each student should have his/her own "tool-box" of skills for planning, managing, and evaluating the language-learning process.

Centering Your Learning: Review a key concept or principle and link it to already existing knowledge, make a firm decision to pay attention to the general concept, ignore input that is distracting, and learn skills in the proper order.

Arranging and Planning Your Learning: The following strategies help the learner maximize the learning experience: take the time to understand how a language is learned; create optimal learning conditions, i.e., regulate noise, lighting and temperature; obtain the appropriate books, etc.; and set reasonable long-term and short-term goals.

Evaluate Your Learning: The following strategies help learners assess their learning achievements: keep track of errors that prevent further progress and keep track of progress, e.g., reading faster now than the previous month.

Socioaffective Strategies

(a) *Affective strategies* are those that help the learner to control the emotions and attitudes that hinder progress in learning the second language and at the same time learn to interact in a social environment. Socioaffective strategies are broken down into "affective" and "social" strategies. There are three sets of affective strategies: "Lowering Your Anxiety," "Encouraging Yourself," and "Taking Your Emotional Temperature," which are easily remembered with the acronym LET.

- Lowering Your Anxiety: These strategies try to maintain emotional equilibrium with physical activities: use meditation and/or deep breathing to relax, listen to calming music, and read a funny book or watch a comedy.

- Encourage Yourself: These strategies help support and self-motivate the learner. Stay positive through self-affirmations, take risks, and give yourself rewards.

- Take Your Emotional Temperature: These strategies help learners control their emotions by understanding what they are feeling emotionally, as well as why they are feeling that way. Listen to body signals; create a checklist to keep track of feelings and motivations during the second-language-acquisition process; keep a diary to record progress and feelings; and share feelings with a classmate or friend.

(b) *Social strategies* affect how the learner interacts in a social setting. The following are three useful strategies for interacting socially: asking questions, cooperating with others, and empathizing with others, which can be remembered by the acronym ACE.

- Asking Questions: Ask for clarification or help. Request that the speaker slow down, repeat, paraphrase, etc., and ask to be corrected when you are speaking.

- Cooperate with Others: Interact with more than one person: work cooperatively with a partner or small group and work with a native speaker of the language.

- Empathizing with Others: Learn how to relate to others, remembering that people usually have more aspects in common than differences. Empathize with another student by learning about his/her culture and being aware and sensitive to the thoughts and feelings of others. Perhaps a fellow student is sad because of something that has happened. Understanding and emphasizing will help that student but it will also help the empathizer.

SKILL 3.7 **Recognize the role of feedback in language development and demonstrate knowledge of strategies for appropriately monitoring ELL students' language errors and for addressing ELL students' needs**

Ur (1996) defines feedback as "information given to the learner about his or her performance of a learning task, usually with the objective of improving this performance." This can be as simple as a thumbs-up, a grade of 75% on a quiz or test, a raised eyebrow when the student makes a mistake, or comments in the margin of an essay.

Feedback has two main aspects: assessment and correction. Typically, a grade assigned on a written paper, saying 'No' to an oral response, simply calling on another student, or a comment such as 'Fair' at the end of a written paragraph are used in the language classroom as ways of assessing performance. In correction, comments on a specific aspect of the ELL's performance are given: better or additional alternatives may be suggested, an explanation of why the ELL's answer is incorrect or partially correct may be given, or the teacher may elicit a better response from the student.

Research suggests that not all errors need correcting. Different theories look at mistakes in different ways:

- Audio-lingualism: Learners should make few mistakes because they learn in small, controlled steps, so corrections are meaningless.
- Interlanguage: Mistakes are an important factor in language learning; by correcting them the learner's interlanguage approaches the target language. (Selinker, 1972, 1992).
- Communicative approach: Not all mistakes need to be corrected. Correct only those mistakes that interfere with meaning.
- Monitor theory: Correction does not lead to language acquisition. Learners need comprehensible input so that they can acquire the target language. (Krashen, 1982).

COMPETENCY 4.0 **Understand cognitive, affective, sociocultural, and other variables that affect second language learning and how to apply this knowledge to facilitate the process of learning English as a new language.**

SKILL 4.1 **Demonstrate knowledge of cognitive variables that affect L2 acquisition (e.g., cognitive development, memory, planning and organizational skills) and recognize the importance of using instructional strategies that are developmentally appropriate, promote critical thinking and problem solving, and address students' specific cognitive strengths and needs**

Cognitive processes are used by the learner to organize and direct second language acquisition. Examples of these processes are: problem-solving, methods of approaching the learning of new information; choices regarding what to ignore and what to pay attention to (Díaz-Rico, Weed, 1995). Developing these skills leads to language acquisition, but they also bridge languages and serve to enhance cognitive skills in the first language.

Research demonstrates that learning and using more than one language

- enhances problem solving and analytical skills.
- allows better formation of concepts.
- increases visual-social abilities.
- furthers logical reasoning.
- supports cognitive flexibility.

Cognitive skills are any mental skills that are used in the process of acquiring knowledge, including reasoning, perception, and intuition. Using these skills in second language learning applies L2 vocabulary and sentence patterns to thought processes that have already formed in the L1.

Memorizing the words and rules of a second language is insufficient to integrate the second language into the learner's thought patterns. L2 learners use cognitive processes to form rules, which allow them to understand and create novel utterances. The creation of novel utterances, whether grammatically correct or not, offers proof that the L2 learner is not simply mimicking chunks of prescribed language, but rather is using cognitive processes to acquire the second language. People use their own thinking processes, or cognition, to discover the rules of the language they are acquiring.

Planning what actions to take when confronted with an academic or social challenge demonstrates understanding of the problem and the ability to confront it. By engaging the cognitive skills, the student can plan where and how to search for information, how to organize it and how to present the information for review.

Organizational Skills may show differences in different cultural contexts. For example, when organizing information for writing, the English speaker normally goes from a smaller unit to a larger unit. In addresses, for example: Dr. Randal Price/ Department of English as a Second Language/ University of Georgia/Athens, Ga./USA. A Japanese speaker would begin with the larger unit and go to the smaller one. For example: USA/Athens, Ga. /University of Georgia/Department of English as a Second Language/Dr. Randal Price. Teachers cannot assume their students know these skills. Even the most basic organizational skill concepts must be glossed or fully taught if necessary.

SKILL 4.2 **Demonstrate knowledge of affective variables that affect L2 acquisition (e.g., inhibition, motivation, self-esteem) and strategies for applying this knowledge to facilitate the process of learning English as a new language**

The term **affective domain** refers to the range of feelings and emotions in human behavior that affects how a second language is acquired. Self-esteem, motivation, anxiety, and attitude all contribute to the second language acquisition process. Internal and external factors influence the affective domain. ESOL teachers must be aware of each student's personality and must stay especially attuned to the affective factors in their students.

Self-Esteem: Learning a second language puts learners in a vulnerable frame of mind. While some learners are less inhibited about taking risks, all learners can easily be shut down if their comfort level is surpassed. Using teaching techniques that lower stress and emphasize group participation rather than focusing on individuals getting the right answer reduce anxiety and encourage learners to attempt to use the new language.

Motivation: Researchers Gardner and Lambert (1972) have identified two types of motivation in relation to learning a second language:

- **Instrumental Motivation:** acquiring a second language for a specific reason, such as a job
- **Integrative Motivation:** acquiring a second language to fulfill a wish to communicate within a different culture

Neither type stands completely alone. Instructors recognize that motivation can be viewed as either a "trait" or a "state." As a trait, motivation is more permanent and culturally acquired. As a state, motivation is considered temporary because it fluctuates, depending on rewards and penalties.

Anxiety: Anxiety is inherent in second-language learning. Students are required to take risks, such as speaking in front of their peers. Without a native's grasp of the language, second language learners are unable to express their individuality, which is even more threatening and uncomfortable. However, not all anxiety is debilitative. Bailey's (1983) research on "facilitative anxiety" (anxiety that compels an individual to stay on task) is a positive factor for some learners, closely related to competitiveness.

Attitudes: Attitude typically evolves from internalized feelings about oneself and one's ability to learn a language. On the other hand, one's attitude about language and the speakers of that language is largely external and influenced by the surrounding environment of classmates and family.

If non-native speakers of English experience discrimination because of their accents or cultural status, their attitude toward the value of second language learning may diminish. Schools can significantly improve the attitude towards second language learners by encouraging activities between native speakers and ELLs. This can be particularly beneficial to both groups if students learning the ELL's first language work on projects together. When native speakers get a chance to appreciate the ELL's language skill in their first language, attitudes change and ELLs have an opportunity to shine.

In some cultures, children who learn a second language at the expense of their primary language might be viewed as "turncoats" by family and friends. This can cause negative feelings about school in general and can adversely affect second language acquisition.

SKILL 4.3   Demonstrate knowledge of sociocultural and political variables that affect L2 acquisition (e.g., idioms; variations in register, dialect, and language genre; factors related to immigration, cultural transition, prior educational background and opportunities; socioeconomic and legal status) and strategies for applying this knowledge to facilitate the process of learning English as a new language

Social factors such as gender, social status, age, occupation, and educational level have an impact on second language acquisition. How learners perceive themselves and what opportunities are available to them influence their attitudes toward education, as well as what they are able to achieve academically.

Gender influences second language acquisition, particularly of English. Typically, families who immigrate to the United States, bring with them their experience of gender roles. Depending on the country, strict cultural norms can diminish the role of the woman, while placing a higher regard on the man. Countries such as China value males more highly than females. When Chinese families immigrate to the United States, existing sexist attitudes towards the female may still prevail, regardless of the new culture's attitudes toward gender equality. As a result, the family may focus on and be very supportive of the education of a son, placing little emphasis on a daughter's education. Many cultures, including many Hispanic countries, value the traditional role of women as mothers and homemakers. Many Hispanic families feel that education goes against what they want for their daughters and will not allow them to continue with higher education.

Social class or status can also heavily influence second language acquisition, as some countries hold strong beliefs as to whether an individual can rise above their intended station in life. India is a prime example of a highly stratified society. Indians believe in a caste system that prohibits individuals from moving beyond their original social class, unlike the United States, where the Constitution guarantees "life, liberty and the pursuit of happiness" to each of its citizens. While many people in the U. S. believe education is the key to higher paying jobs and economic security, this sentiment is not embraced by some groups, such as the young male population born in St. Croix. They believe that the educational system "subjugates", rather than "educates." These men share a commonly held belief that the social position of their family, rather than academic achievement, ensures economic prosperity and power (Gibson, 1991a).

Age can impact second language acquisition when a culture determines what a person does, as well as when they can do it. For example, as noted by Sindell (1988), middle-class European Americans tend to expect that children will play and behave appropriately for their age, rather than take on more adult responsibilities. In contrast, young Cree Indian children are expected to carry out many adult responsibilities. Furthermore, many Cree Indian parents disapprove of academic activities because they distract the children from involvement in the Cree Indian society.

Occupation, especially in the United States, often determines one's economic status, level of prestige, and amount of power and influence. However, in other countries, regardless of how much one earns, the type of power and prestige available may largely depend on family connections or position within the dominant religious establishment. Learner perceptions of occupations, i.e., whether a certain position is of interest or even feasible, affects second language acquisition. If education is not viewed as a realistic pathway to careers and economic security, then academic success and L2 proficiency become less of a priority.

A family's educational level has a profound impact on second language acquisition, and may determine what kind of academic achievement and investment an L2 learner is going make. A learner who comes from a family in which no one advanced beyond elementary school likely has little knowledge about what types of careers are available or how one studies and advances. One cannot aspire to something to which one has not been exposed. Each higher level of academic achievement dramatically increases the number and variety of occupational choices, as well as the lifetime earnings a person can expect, particularly in the United States. For ELLs who expect to return to their native country or to follow that culture's traditions, this provides little incentive to take language learning seriously.

SKILL 4.4   Demonstrate knowledge of individual variables that affect L2 acquisition (e.g., age, level of L1 language proficiency, level of L1 literacy, personality, preferred learning styles and modalities, educational experience, disabilities)

Age
According to Ellis (1985), age does not affect the 'route' (order) of second language acquisition (SLA). Thus, children and adults acquire language in the same order, that is, go through the same stages. With respect to rate of acquisition, teens appear to surpass both children and adults, especially in learning the grammatical system (Snow & Hoefnagel-Hohle, 1978). Older learners seem to be more efficient learners. The achievement of a foreign language is strongly related to the amount of time spent on the language, and the earlier a second language is started, the better the pronunciation (Burstall et al., 1974). Krashen (1982) disagrees, believing instead that SLA is related to the amount of comprehensible input (i.e. the younger child will receive more comprehensible input) and that younger learners are more open emotionally to SLA.

Other theorists have formulated different hypotheses about age in SLA related to affective factors. In the Critical Period Hypothesis, Penfield and Roberts (1959) state that the first 10 years are the best age for SLA as the brain retains its plasticity. After puberty, this plasticity disappears and the flexibility required for SLA is lost. Guiora et al., (1972) believe that around the age of puberty, the ability to acquire native-like pronunciation of the foreign language is no longer present.

Cognitive explanations are also used to explain the effects of age on SLA. These theories believe that children are more prone to use their Language Acquisition Device (LAD), while adults are better able to use their inductive reasoning because of more fully developed cognitive faculties. Rosansky (1975) explains SLA in terms of Piaget's "period of concrete operations." Rosansky believes the child is more open and flexible to new language than an adult who identifies more closely with the differences in the native language and the language to be acquired. Krashen (1982) believes that adolescents and adults probably have greater access to comprehensible input than children and that this is the real causative variable, rather than age itself.

Level of L1 language proficiency

Children who are just beginning their education may be able to stay in the general classroom for instruction while older children may need to have specific language items (such as phonemes, syntax, pragmatics, and lexis) taught in specialized classes that take advantage of L1 while teaching the content areas. Nevertheless, McLaughlin (1990) states that the more proficient a learner is in L1, the more the learner understands about language structures and the better he or she is able to use that knowledge to help make language choices when communicating in L2.

Level of L1 literacy

Cummins' (1981) Interdependence Hypothesis claimed that the degree of knowledge and skill evident in L1 will determine the ease of transfer to L2. Thus, it will take a student who has L1 proficiency but is only an emergent reader in L1 longer to achieve proficiency in the L2 than a student who is orally proficient in his or her L1 and in L1 reading ability.

Personality

It isn't clear from research whether or not **extroversion or introversion** affects second language learning. It has been assumed that extroversion leads to better L2 acquisition, but confusing definitions in defining the different competencies make this unclear. However, it is generally assumed that extroverted students are chattier and develop more communicative competence. Entwhistle and Entwhistle (1970) found that introverted students developed better study habits and had high overall language proficiency.

Despite inconclusive evidence, **tolerance of ambiguity** is considered another trait of a good language learner. Budner (1964) developed a scale to define the language learner as one who is comfortable in novel, complex, or insoluble situations (tolerance of ambiguity), or one who perceives these situations as a threat (intolerance of ambiguity). Naiman et al., (1978), using Budner's scale, claimed that tolerance of ambiguity correlated to listening comprehension scores but not with imitation test scores.

Another personality trait which affects language learning is **anxiety.** MacIntyre and Gardner (1987) believe that anxiety affects the three main stages involved in language learning: input, processing, and output. Scovel (1978) studied the distinction between facilitating and debilitating anxiety. Facilitating anxiety helps the learner because the learner wants to do well and succeed while debilitating anxiety limits or holds the learner back from performing well because they cannot help themselves.

The effects of **risk taking and inhibition** similarly have conflicting evidence with regard to their effect on language learning. McClelland et al., (1953) found that risk taking is necessary to rapid progress in L2. Krashen (1981) maintains that the Affective Filter develops as adolescents reach puberty; therefore, they become more self-conscious and less willing to take risks than younger children. Other studies show similar results. Still, the instructor needs to be aware that most of this research was done in psychological laboratories and involves out-of-context behavior with tasks of no practical significance for language learners. Consequently, this research may be of questionable validity.

While an ELL's personality traits are probably unchangeable, the teacher can still encourage certain attitudes towards language learning that possibly could have a positive effect on the ELL's personality profile.

- Respect for the target language (TL), TL speakers, and TL culture
- Emphasis on the practical and positive aspects of language learning
- Confidence in the teacher

Preferred learning styles and modalities
A student's learning style includes cognitive, affective and psychological behaviors that indicate the learner's characteristic and consistent way of perceiving, interacting with and responding to the learning environment (Willing, 1988).

Willing (1988) identified four main learning styles used by ESL learners in Australia

- Concrete learning style: people-oriented, emotional and spontaneous
- Analytic learning style: object-orientated, with capacity for making connections and inferences
- Communicative learning style: autonomous, prefers social learning, likes making decisions
- Authority-orientated learning style: defers to the teacher, does not enjoy learning by discovery, intolerant of facts that do not fit (ambiguity)

Reid (1987) identified four perceptual learning tendencies:

- Visual learning: learning mainly from seeing words in books, on the board, etc.
- Auditory learning: learning by hearing words spoken and from oral explanations, from listening to tapes or to lectures
- Kinesthetic learning: learning by experience, by being involved physically in classroom experiences
- Tactile learning: hands on learning, learning by doing, working on models, lab experiments, etc.

Educational experience

ELLs come to the United States for many different reasons: a better life, fleeing war zones, oppressive governments, or economic difficulties. In many cases, ELLs have entered the school system in their native land and done very well. In other cases, the ELLs have had little or no educational experience. In both cases, it is imperative that previous to or upon enrollment, assessment of the student take place—if possible in their L1. By building on their previous knowledge with regard to literacy, language, and experience, L2 instruction will be more successful (Au, 1993, 2002; Ovando et al., 2006).

Shumm (2006) emphasizes that not only are the reading level characteristics important, but also the differences between L1 and L2, as these may influence the assumed level of the student. Some of the questions she proposes to elicit these similarities and differences are useful for further evaluation of reading level characteristics:

- Is the L1 writing system logographic as is Arabic, syllabic as is Cherokee, or alphabetic as are English and Greek?
- How does the L1 syntax compare with L2's?
- Are the spelling patterns phonetic with consistent grapheme-phoneme relationships (e.g. Spanish or French), or are there multiple vowel sounds (e.g. English)?
- Do students read from left to right and top to bottom in their L1?
- Are there true cognates (Spanish: instrucción and English: instruction) and false cognates (Spanish: librería <bookstore> and English: library) that will help or confuse the ELL?
- Are the discourse patterns and writing styles of L1 and L2 similar or different?
- Are questions with known answers asked (teacher questions) or are rhetorical questions (found among many working class families) asked?
- Is L1 writing style circular, with long sentences and many details (e.g. Spanish) or linear, with the minimum number of facts or supporting details needed to support the main idea (e.g. English)?

Disabilities

Students with disabilities are guaranteed an education under Public Law 94-142 of 1975. A key feature of the law is the requirement for an individualized educational program (IEP) for any student receiving special funds for special education. This said, the classification of many ELLs or the "dumping" of ELLs in special education classes has been of concern to many educators. Those testing ELLs for placement in different classes must be certain that the tests used are both reliable and valid. Reliability can be established using multiple assessment measures, objective tests, multiple raters, and clearly specified scoring criteria (Valdez-Pierce, 2003). For a test to be valid, it must first be reliable (Goh, 2004).

Learning disabilities refer to physical, emotional, cognitive, or social components, which severely limits what is considered to be "normal" functioning behavior. Children who fall into this category can be one or more of the following: emotionally challenged, hearing, vision or speech impaired, and/or learning disabled, etc.

Some of the similarities between second language development and learning disabilities are the following:

Similarities:
Educators have numerous assessment tools to evaluate the proficiency level of an L2 learner. They also have various assessment tools to determine if an L1 learner has a disability, whether it is physical, emotional or learning. However, assessment tools to determine whether an L2 learner has a learning disability are not currently available. The most reliable method to date is that of observation and interpretation.

The typical blueprint, which L2 learners seem to follow in terms of developing their pronunciation skills, can be easily confused with a learning disability, because both groups of learners have difficulties in the following areas: omission, substitution, distortion and addition (Lue, 2001). And, off course, there are some L2 learners with learning disabilities. The following are examples of the problem areas:

Omission: The L1/L2 learner omits a phoneme (the smallest unit of a word). For example: the L1/L2 learner pronounces "_ar" instead of "bar."

Substitution: The L1/L2 learner substitutes a phoneme. For example: the L1/L2 learner pronounces "take" instead of "rake."

Distortion: The L1/L2 learner pronounces a phoneme incorrectly, and the sound produced is not considered normal. For example: the L1/L2 learner pronounces the phoneme "three" as "free."

Addition: The L1/L2 learner adds an additional syllable to a word. For example, when a learner pronounces the word "liked" as "like-id", this is an addition.

SKILL 4.5   Demonstrate knowledge of linguistic variables that affect L2 acquisition (e.g., difficulty level of language structures and vocabulary) and apply knowledge of strategies for developing ELL students' social and academic language proficiency in English

Research demonstrates that language learners acquire (or learn) language as they are ready to process it. According to different theories, a student's **interlanguage** is the language a student develops that is somewhere between L1 and L2. The interlanguage can be visualized as a midpoint on a continuum between L1 and L2 or it may be represented by a Venn diagram. This interlanguage changes as the ELL learns more of the L2 structure and approaches native language fluency.

Language is not acquired lineally, but is influenced by individual factors such as age, personality, educational background, previous L1 and L2 language experience, context, etc.). Contradictions in SLA may be explained by Long's (1990) Backsliding Theory or the so-called U-shaped Behavior. More recently, Larsen-Freeman (1997) refers to this period as a period of randomness and suggests that Chaos Theory offers the most satisfactory representation of the seemingly unstable system of second language learning.

Teachers often follow the Presentation, Practice, and Production (PPP) model. In this model, teachers present small amounts of language, give the ELLs the opportunity to practice the items, and later integrate the items into other language in order to acquire communication (production). Bearing in mind the previous theories, items should be re-taught and recycled at frequent intervals for the ELLs to firmly acquire the needed language items and make them a solid part of their language skills.

SUBAREA 2.0   ESOL CULTURAL AND PROFESSIONAL ENVIRONMENTS

COMPETENCY 5.0   Understand major concepts, principal theories, and research related to the nature of culture, sociocultural systems, and the role of culture in language development and learning.

SKILL 5.1   Demonstrate knowledge of major cultural concepts (e.g., cultural relativism, cultural universalism, intra- and intergroup differences, acculturation, assimilation, accommodation, biculturalism, the additive nature of culture)

Cultural relativism refers to the principle that a person's beliefs and activities should be understood in the context of his society. This concept is based upon the work of the anthropologist Boas (1887) who wrote: "civilization is not something absolute, but ... is relative, and ... our ideas and conceptions are true only so far as our civilization goes."

Cultural universalism is defined as the elements, patterns, traits, or institutions that are common to all human cultures worldwide. Some anthropologists and sociologists may minimize the importance of the existence of cultural universals, claiming that many of these "cultural" items are in fact biologically inherited behaviors, leading to the "nature vs. nurture" controversy.

Cross-cultural studies focus on **intra-cultural** issues where members of the same culture are involved and **inter-cultural** issues which involve members of different cultures. Examples of inter-culture might be the classroom culture, youth culture, company culture, or disciplinary culture. Even within these limited cultures, there are differences in the intra-culture of their members.

At its most basic level, cultural adaptation is generally considered to be assimilation, acculturation, and accommodation, though social anthropologists have many more definitions with which to describe the very complex phenomena of cultures coming together.

Assimilation is considered to be the process of integration of immigrants or minorities into the predominate culture. This implies a loss for the immigrants of their native culture through changes in language, customs, ethnicity, and self-identity.

The melting pot theory was an attempt to explain the assimilation process in the United States in when it was considered correct to assume that the United States was a homogeneous society, and cultural differences, except physical ones such as skin color, were ignored.

Social scientists use four benchmarks to evaluate the degree of social assimilation: socioeconomic status, geographic distribution, second language attainment, and intermarriage. The degree to which the immigrants or minorities achieve socioeconomic status through education, jobs, and income mark the degree of assimilation. As the immigrant culture becomes assimilated by increased socioeconomic attainment, longer residency in the U.S., and higher generational status, it seems to spread out and move away from the intense concentration of the immigrant culture. Language assimilation is considered to be a three-generation process. The first generation tries to learn the 'new' language but the native tongue remains dominate, the second generation is bilingual, and the third generation loses their "native" language, speaking only the language of the new country. High rates of intermarriage are presumed to be strong indicators of social integration because intermarriage reduces the capacity of families to pass on one consistent culture and thus intermarriage becomes an agent of assimilation.

Acculturation is the process of becoming accustomed to the customs, language, practices, and environment of a new culture. The factors that influence this process include, but are not limited to, the learner's desire and ability to become a part of the dominant culture.

Acculturation occurs when two distinct cultures come in contact, altering the original cultural patterns of either or both groups. The cultural groups remain distinct. Definitions and evidence of acculturation state that this is a two-way process, but research and theory continue to explore the adjustments and changes that the aboriginal peoples, immigrants, and other minorities experience when in contact with the dominant culture. Thus, acculturation is believed to be the process by which cultural learning is imposed upon the weaker cultures simply because they are weaker. Acculturation then becomes a process of learning a second culture and the minority culture becomes displaced. Transculturation is acculturation by an individual while acculturation is the same process for a large group.

Accommodation theory emerged in the 1970s as an explanation of motivations underlying, and the consequences of, adapting our language and communication patterns to others. Since its emergence, it has been used in a wide variety of disciplines and has been expanded many times. It can be used to facilitate or impede second language learning as well as to refer to immigrants' acceptance into host communities. Teachers can facilitate language learning by accommodating their language—vocabulary, structure, and pronunciation—to make it more comprehensible for those who are striving for proficiency. Immigrant groups or ethnic groups accommodate their cultural heritage to the host or dominant culture in an effort to show their flexibility and willingness to assimilate.

Biculturalism is often adopted in countries with a history of national or ethnic conflict where neither side has obtained a complete victory. The conflict may be between colonizers and indigenous people(s) or between rival groups of colonizers. The term was first used in the Canadian context. Examples in the United States are the biculturalism that exists between the U.S. and Mexico or between the U.S. and its Afro-American citizens.

The **additive nature of culture**: Ong (1982) claimed that in oral societies many things were happening at once—socialization played a great role in the operation of these cultures. Memory and memorization were of greater importance, increasing the amount of copiousness and redundancy. Oral cultures were additive rather than subordinate, closer to the real life world, and more situational and participatory than the more abstract literate cultures.

SKILL 5.2 Demonstrate knowledge of the interrelationship between language and culture and the effects of this interrelationship on ELL students' language development and learning

While there is a continuous effort to establish a "Standard English" to be taught for English Language Learners (ELLs), English learning and acquisition depends on the cultural and linguistic background of the ELL, as well as preconceived perceptions of English language cultural influences. These factors can act as a filter, causing confusion and inhibiting learning. Since language by definition is an attempt to share knowledge, the cultural, ethnic, and linguistic diversity of learners influences both their own history as well as how they approach and learn a new language.

Teachers must assess the ELL to determine how cultural, ethnic, and linguistic experience can impact the student's learning. This evaluation should take into account many factors, including:

- the cultural background and educational sophistication of the ELL
- the exposure of the ELL to various English language variants and cultural beliefs.

No single approach, program, or set of practices fits all students' needs, backgrounds, and experiences. The ideal program for a Native American teenager attending an isolated tribal school may fail to reach a Hispanic youth enrolled in an inner-city or suburban district.

Culture encompasses the sum of human activity and symbolic structures that have significance and importance for a particular group of people. Culture is manifested in language, customs, history, arts, beliefs, institutions and other representative characteristics, and is a means of understanding the lives and actions of people.

Customs play an important part in language learning because they directly affect interpersonal exchanges. What is polite in one culture might be offensive in another. For example, in the U. S., making direct eye contact is considered polite. Refusing to make eye contact connotes deviousness, inattention, or rude behavior. The custom in many Asian cultures is exactly the opposite. Teachers who are unaware of this cultural difference can easily offend an Asian ELL and unwittingly cause a barrier to learning. However, teachers who are familiar with this custom can make efforts not to offend the learner and can teach the difference between the two customs so that the ELL can learn how to interact without allowing contrary customs to interfere.

Beliefs and institutions have a strong emotional influence on ELLs and should always be respected. While customs should be adaptable, similar to switching registers when speaking, no effort should be made to change the beliefs or institutional values of an ELL. Encountering new ideas is a part of growth, learning, and understanding. Even though the beliefs and values of different cultures often have irreconcilable differences, they should be addressed. In these instances teachers must respect alternative attitudes and adopt an "agree to disagree" attitude. Presenting new, contrasting points of view should not be avoided, because new ideas can strengthen original thinking as well as change it. All presentations should be neutral, however, and no effort should be made to alter a learner's thinking. While addressing individual cultural differences, teachers should also teach tolerance of all cultures. This is especially important in a culturally diverse classroom, but will serve all students well in their future interactions.

Studying the **history and various art forms** of a culture reveals much about the culture and offers opportunities to tap into the interests and talents of ELLs. Comparing the history and art of different cultures encourages critical thinking and often reveals commonalities as well as differences, leading to greater understanding among people.

Culture constitutes a rich component of language learning. It offers a means of drawing learners into the learning process and greatly expands their understanding of a new culture, as well as their own. Second language acquisition, according to the findings of Saville-Troike (1986) places the learner in the position of having to learn a "second culture." The outcome of learning a second culture can have negative or positive results, depending not only upon how teaching is approached, but also upon outside factors. How people in the new culture respond to ELLs makes them feel welcome or rejected. The attitudes and behavior of the learner's family are particularly important. If the family is supportive and embraces the second culture, the effect is typically positive. However, if acculturation is perceived as rejecting the primary culture, then the child risks feeling alienated from both cultures.

SKILL 5.3 **Demonstrate knowledge of the content of culture and sociocultural systems (e.g., values, beliefs, and expectations; roles and status; family structure, function, and socialization; humanities and the arts; assumptions about literacy and other content areas; communication and communication systems) and their effects on learning and cross-cultural interactions**

There are many different ways that students are affected by the **cultural differences** in their native culture and home when compared with the culture being acquired through schooling and daily life in a foreign culture.

The following points, adapted from Peregoy and Boyle (2008), illustrate some of the many different ways that culture affects us daily and thus affects students in their participation, learning, and adjustment to a different society and its schools.

- **Family structures:**
  What constitutes a family? What are the rights and responsibilities of each family member? What is the hierarchy of authority?

- **Life cycles:**
  What are the criteria for defining stages, periods, or transitions in life? What rites of passage are there? What behaviors are considered appropriate for children of different ages? How might these conflict with behaviors taught or encouraged in school?

- **Roles and interpersonal relationships:**
  How do the roles of girls and women differ from those of boys and men? How do people greet each other? Do girls work and interact with boys? Is deference shown and to whom and by whom?

- **Discipline:**
  What is discipline? Which behaviors are considered socially acceptable for boys versus girls at different ages? Who or what is considered responsible if a child misbehaves? The child? Parents? Older siblings? The environment? Is blame even ascribed? Who has authority over whom? How is behavior traditionally controlled? To what extent and in what domains?

- **Time and space:**
  How important is punctuality? How important is speed in completing a task? How much space are people accustomed to? What significance is associated with different cultural locations or directions, including north, south, east, and west?

- **Religion:**
  What restrictions are there on topics discussed in school? Are dietary restrictions to be observed, including fasting? What restrictions are associated with death and the dead?

- **Food:**
  What is eaten? In what order and how often is food eaten? Which foods are restricted? Which foods are typical? What social obligations are there with regard to food giving, reciprocity, and honoring people? What restrictions or proscriptions are associated with handling, offering, or discarding food?

- **Health and hygiene:**
  How are illnesses treated and by whom? What is considered the cause of illness? If a student were involved in an accident at school, would any of the common first aid practices be unacceptable?

- **History, traditions, and holidays:**
  Which events and people are sources of pride for this group? To what extent does the group in the United States identify with the history and traditions of the country of origin? What holidays and celebrations are considered appropriate for observing in school? Which ones are appropriate for private observance?

SKILL 5.4 **Demonstrate knowledge of the process of cultural contact and stages or phases of acculturation (e.g., characteristics of culture shock)**

Culture concerns the shared beliefs, values and rule-governed patterns of behavior, including language, which define a group and are required for group membership (Goodenough, 1981; Saville-Troike, 1978). **Cultural adjustment** occurs when people from different cultures are subjected to changes in these beliefs, habits, and customs. These changes may come because the person has fled their country or left it permanently in an effort to seek better educational, financial or cultural opportunities. Many others choose to leave their native land and become part of a foreign culture. There are four generally recognized stages of acculturation:

- **The Honeymoon Stage:**
  Everything looks bright and positive. The individual or family have arrived in their new land and are ready to begin a new era in their life. Everyone is eager to please, ready to interact, and happy to be in their new home.

- **The Hostility Stage:**
  Frustration begins to occur as reality strikes. The new language, the new survival tasks (dealing with subways or buses), new foods, and new ways of doing things at work or at school are unfamiliar and viewed as problems with the new society. Depression, anger, anxiety, and "homesickness" are felt during this phase.

- **The Humor Stage:**
  Accomplishments bring on a triumphant feeling that the new society might not be so bad. As the individuals or families experience success and adjust to life's new demands, they are able to laugh at themselves and their previous frustrations.

- **The Home Stage:**
  Patriotism to the native country is retained while accepting the new country as the new home. A transition from the old to the new norms has occurred and the new location is seen as home.

The length of time of each stage depends on the individual and may be shortened by positive experiences within the individual's circle of contacts.

SKILL 5.5 **Recognize the role of culture in the classroom and school (e.g., effects of the degree of cultural congruence between ELL students' home cultures and the school culture) and demonstrate knowledge of cultural differences in approaches to learning (e.g., cooperation versus competition, visual/holistic versus verbal/linear-sequential, individual versus group)**

Teachers are both participants and observers in their classrooms. As such, they are in a unique position to observe what makes their students uncomfortable. By writing these observations in a teaching journal, the teacher can begin to note what activities and topics make the students in her classroom uncomfortable. Does this discomfort come from multicultural insensitivity?

Another method of **demonstrating sensitivity** is to use appropriate "teacher talk" in the classroom. Wait time for student response differs in different cultures. Too, students who are struggling to formulate their answers may need more time than the teacher normally gives for responding. Also, if the questions are rhetorical, students may be reluctant to answer them, as they see no point to such a question.

Cooperative group work is based on the premise that many cultures are more comfortable working in collaborative groups. However, while this is true, many students may feel that the teacher is the only academic authority in the classroom and as such, should answer questions rather than their peers. Different students feel more comfortable with different instructional formats, due to both cultural and individual preferences. By balancing group work with teacher-directed instruction, both points of view should be accommodated.

Literacy and reading instruction are areas where multicultural sensitivity can be increased in the classroom regardless of the level of the students. Many immigrant children arrive in the classroom with few, if any, literacy skills. They may not have had the opportunity to go to school. Others may be fully literate, with substantial prior education. In both cases, reading materials that are culturally sensitive are necessary for the students, both native English speakers and ELLs, to have the opportunity to discuss the ways in which different cultures are alike and different. Oral discussion of books will provide opportunities for comprehensible input and negotiation of meaning.

Research has shown that the key to any reading program is extensive reading (Day & Bamford, 1998; Krashen, 1993). Advantages include building vocabulary and background knowledge, interest in reading, and improved comprehension. For the multicultural classroom, it is important to provide culturally sensitive materials. Avoid materials which distort or omit certain historical events, portray stereotyping, contain loaded words, use speech that is culturally offensive, portrays gender roles, elders and family inaccurately, or distorts or offends a student's self-image. All materials should be of high literary quality.

Show and Tell is another strategy for raising multicultural sensitivity. Students of all ages can bring in objects from their home cultures and tell the class about their uses, where they are from, how they are made, and so on.

Misunderstandings can be worked into the classroom by asking students to share an incident that involved cultural misunderstanding. Questions can be asked about the nature of the misunderstanding—what was involved: words, body language, social customs, or stereotypes.

Visual/holistic versus verbal/linear-sequential: Not all learners learn in the same manner. Some students learn best through seeing information—whether written text, charts, pictures, or flow chart—visually. Other students prefer to hear the message spoken by a teacher or other students. Still other students learn best through tactile experiences, e.g. manipulating objects or equipment, creating models, or presenting material through art or drama.

According to Cassidy (2004),The holistic-analytical dimension concerns the way in which individuals tend to process information, either as a whole (holistic) or broken down into parts (analytic). Riding and Cheema (1991 in Cassidy 2004) determined that the holistic-analytical learner is commonly associated with the following terms: analytic-deductive, rigorous, constrained, convergent, formal, critical and synthetic. The verbalizer-imager concerns the way in which individuals tend to represent information either as words or as images (Cassidy 2004).

Teachers need to be aware of the different ways in which students learn so that they can prepare classroom experiences and material which encompass the different learning styles. By presenting materials through different multisensory channels, all students are given an opportunity to learn material through their preferred learning style and to have it reinforced in other ways.

COMPETENCY 6.0   **Understand characteristic features of cultures, the effect of ELL students' cultural identities on language development and learning, and teaching strategies that are sensitive to the needs of ELL students from diverse cultural groups**

SKILL 6.1   **Recognize how to use a variety of print and nonprint resources to learn about world cultures and the diverse cultures of students, including characteristic features of linguistic-minority cultures**

The term culture is problematic in that culture has many possible meanings. Culture may be seen in the aesthetic sense, the sociological sense, the semantic sense, and the pragmatic sense. For students of diverse cultures to learn about other world cultures represents a huge challenge, yet it is the only way to deal with many of the everyday issues in the language classroom.

Literature is one way to learn about other cultures. The story often describes the culture, its setting, and the customs of the characters. Film oftentimes captures the essence of diverse cultures while presenting them in a visual format. "Australia" (2008) and "Slumdog Millionaire" (2008) portray cultural aspects of Australia and India, respectively. For younger students, picture books or short videos can serve the same purpose.

ELLs (as well as their classmates) can bring special items of their culture from home for 'show and tell'. A piñata, a Russian tea urn, masks, grass skirts, paintings or their reproductions, etc. are all objects that can be used to explain diverse elements of culture.

The overwhelming influence of English on world cultures is of growing concern to theorists, including those in such influential bodies as the United Nations. Linguistic imperialism and belonging to **linguistic-minority cultures** may cause ELLs to feel disenfranchised when they encounter English in all aspects of their lives. Whether or not they wish to, they must learn English in order to succeed in getting a good education (in many countries, e.g. England, Canada, Australia, and the United States) or getting a good job with a multinational corporation. Even negotiating native or heritage foodstuffs, goods, or services requires a working knowledge of English. Frequently, the only recourse of a linguistic-minority culture is to use it within the limits of the community and adopt the language of the dominant culture in which they are also members.

SKILL 6.2 **Recognize the effects of world events (e.g., U.S. immigration history, patterns, and policies; events in students' home countries) on ELL students and their families**

Large scale migrations have caused world governments to carefully consider what is culture and cultural identity. For many ELLs entering U.S. schools, their cultural identity has been challenged by migration. Political unrest and wars, natural disasters, need for improved living conditions – all contribute to the desire of populations and individuals to migrate to other countries and cultures. In recent U.S. history, one of the most recognized periods of immigration was the third period of migrations from Cuba from December 1965 to April 1973, known as the Freedom Flights that resulted from the fall of Batista (Beebe and Mackey, 1990). Many of these refugees were wealthy, well-educated professionals or businessmen, who as time went on and their hopes of an early return to Cuba diminished, were forced to start or purchase modest businesses. Those without resources were forced into more menial jobs.

The fall of Saigon in April of 1975 led to a wave of immigration from Vietnam. According to Wikipedia, since 1975, over 650,000 Vietnamese people have left Vietnam for the U.S., making Vietnamese the seventh most commonly spoken language in the U.S. Because of strong U.S. government support of the immigration of Vietnamese to the U.S., President Gerald Ford signed the Indochina Migration and Refugee Assistance Act in 1975 and Congress passed the Refugee Act of 1980, permitting the early entry of refugees to the U.S. in response to the Vietnamese government's establishment of the Orderly Departure Program (ODP) under the United Nations High Commissioner for Refugees in response to world protest of the former enemy combatants.

These two comparatively recent historical incidents illustrate not only changes in our recent cultural history, but in the lives of those who are forced to make decisions which drastically affect their futures and their children. In modern society, relationships are defined by the family, the school, the workplace, the professional organization, and the church. Each organization has its own power hierarchy, its expected roles and statuses, its characteristics values and beliefs, attitudes and ideologies (Kramsch, 1998). Geographic mobility, professional change, and life experiences may cause people to experience internal conflict with their multiple social identities.

SKILL 6.3   Demonstrate knowledge of strategies for promoting ELL students' understanding of aspects of U.S. culture (e.g., names, food and dining, shopping, games, music, literature, government structure and institutions, citizenship issues), including social conventions (e.g., greetings, letter writing, telephone patterns)

To promote the understanding of the U.S. culture, teachers are limited only by their imagination.

Names:
- Seat the class in a circle. Each student says his or her name, repeating all the names of the students who come before him or her. Excellent as an ice-breaker at the beginning of a course!

Food and dining:
- If you're not up for taking all the class out on a field trip, order in! Have parents bring in different foods and prepare labels to identify each dish. During warm weather, this could be organized as a picnic.
- For reinforcement, create a worksheet with columns for each letter of the alphabet and see how many food items can be listed by the class. (Excellent for team competition at the board!)
- Have students bring in different food processing objects, such as a tortilla press, chopsticks, a tea set, or a paella pan, and discuss how they are used.

Shopping:
- Have the class bring in catalogs or pictures of different items to be purchased. Hand out paper money and set a limit on what can be spent.
- Use the food ads from the newspaper to demonstrate how to buy groceries and to reinforce food names.
- For older students, divide the class into groups. Have them study the ads for different high-tech products and let them negotiate a deal with the salesman or saleswoman, played by a classmate.

Games:
- For young children, teach the classic games of Red Rover, Tag, etc.
- Bring in board games that are age appropriate to the class and instruct the students in how to play. Let the fun begin!

Music:
- Teach a folk song. Then let the students write a parody of it. "On Top of Old Smokey" and its parody "On Top of Spaghetti" are two favorites.
- Let students bring in their favorite music for you to review. Photocopy the lyrics, learn the song, and discuss the meaning.

Literature:

- Hand out examples of your favorite short stories, poems, or a novel which illustrates a particular cultural point. Have the class read it and discuss the particular cultural aspect that the piece illustrates. Watch the film, if possible. The more channels the ELL uses to receive messages, the more likely they are to be understood.
- Have the ELLs tell a story about their native culture in their native tongue—and in English. Discuss the cultural points mentioned—the similarities and the differences. This activity will build confidence and send a strong message about the value of bilingualism.

Government structure and institutions:

Students from many cultures arriving in the U.S. come from areas where the government is highly suspect and not to be trusted. Try to cultivate a trust and respect for these institutions by:

- inviting different government officials to speak about their jobs (If these officials are someone's parents, so much the better.).
- visiting different institutions of interest to the students. Take a poll to see what they are interested in. The courtroom is always a popular choice.

Citizenship issues:

Many students are sophisticated about the status of their visas and citizenship. Others probably aren't, so:

- If possible, invite immigration officials (or someone facilitating paperwork for immigrants) to speak to the class.
- Research different laws and citizenship issues on the Internet.

SKILL 6.4   Demonstrate knowledge of cultural differences in communication styles (e.g., nonverbal elements, turn-taking features) and strategies for applying this knowledge to enhance English language learning

Communication in a culture is not only the language; it also involves gestures, facial expressions, and body stance, among other elements. For the nonverbal elements, the teacher or students can model them. Next, ask the ELLs how to communicate the same message in their culture. For example, the distance between different speakers and the way to indicate the height of a person may be different in different cultures.

In many cultures, children do not speak until called upon; in other cultures, children may shout out an answer as soon as the question is asked. Teaching turn-taking in speaking, the use of materials, and other classroom procedures may be a year-long task.

SKILL 6.5 **Recognize how the cultural identity of individuals affects their language development and learning and acknowledge that levels of cultural identity will vary among ELL students and their teachers and apply knowledge of strategies for providing ELL students with opportunities to use their cultural perspectives to promote learning**

ELLs often feel as if they lose a part of themselves when faced with the complexities of learning a new language and culture. To lessen these feelings of alienation and isolation, including elements of the ELL's culture and previous knowledge only enhances the learning in the English classroom. Including culture study in the classroom may be achieved by having each student do a research project on his or her culture and report back to the class. Culture studies of this nature promote reading, writing, speaking, learning to give presentations, and creating visuals. Should there be more than one student from the same culture, pairs or small groups could be organized. Alternative types of assessment could be used to evaluate the process.

SKILL 6.6 **Analyze the effects of racism, stereotyping, and discrimination on teaching and learning and ways to address these issues purposefully in the classroom (e.g., by promoting an inclusive classroom climate, by designing instruction that reflects anti-bias approaches) and the school community (e.g., recognizing ELL students' language rights)**

Racism, stereotyping and **discrimination** are difficult social issues to address in the classroom, because they are cultural elements that die hard. Even so, teachers are charged with addressing these issues in the classroom, especially when they carry negative connotations. Encouraging an all-inclusive classroom climate where everyone is equal is a start. This is fairly easy when dealing with young children, but with older students, the movie *The Ron Clark Story* (2006) could be used to initiate a discussion of these themes. The movie shows how an idealistic young teacher from North Carolina deals with the problems of racism, stereotyping, and discrimination in his New York City classroom.

Language rights refer to the right of each individual to enjoy the uniquely individual and communal privilege of belonging to a language group by which human beings apprehend the world and one another (Kramsch, 1998: 77).

COMPETENCY 7.0   Understand the historical and research foundations of ESOL programs and current educational trends, issues, policies, and professional practices in ESOL

SKILL 7.1   Demonstrate knowledge of the effects of significant federal and state legislation, court cases, and demographic changes on the evolution of ESOL programs

Several legal precedents have established that schools must provide equal educational opportunities for ELLs. This has led directly to improved language instruction and accommodations for language deficiencies. The **Civil Rights Act of 1964** established that schools, as recipients of federal funds, cannot discriminate against ELLs: "No person in the United States shall, on the grounds of race, color, or national origin, be excluded from participation in, be denied the benefits of, or be subjected to discrimination under any program or activity receiving federal financial assistance."

In 1970, this mandate was detailed more specifically for ELLs in the **May 25 Memorandum**: "Where inability to speak and understand the English language excludes national origin-minority group children from effective participation in the educational program offered by a school district, the district must take affirmative steps to rectify the language deficiency in order to open its instructional program to these students." The memorandum specifically addressed the practice of placing ELLs, based on their English language skills, in classes with mentally retarded students, excluding them from college preparatory classes, and failing to notify parents of ELLs of school activities, even if translation is required.

In 1974 the Supreme Court offered a unanimous ruling in **Lau v. Nichols** which established the Lau Plan, which provided specific requirements that schools must meet. Each school must

- meet legal criteria for programming
- form/convene a Language Assessment Committee
- outline staff responsibilities and credentials for instruction
- identify assessment/evaluative tools for ongoing assessment
- set program criteria (entrance/exit standards)
- set parameters for ELL student transition and monitoring
- determine program effectiveness

Schools could no longer merely provide all students with the same facilities, textbooks, teachers, and curriculum. In this ruling the Supreme Court recognized that students who do not understand English are effectively excluded from any meaningful education.

- In a later decision, **Castaneda v. Pickard** (filed in 1978 but not settled until 1981), a federal court established three specific criteria schools must use to determine the effectiveness of bilingual education programs:
- A program for English language learners must be based on pedagogically sound educational theory that is recognized by experts in the field.
- The program must be implemented effectively with resources provided for personnel, instructional materials, and space.
- The program must produce results that indicate the language barrier is being overcome.

The 1983 **A Nation at Risk** report, produced by the National Commission on Excellence in Education, concluded that the U. S. educational system was failing to meet the national need for a competitive workforce. This prompted a flurry of education reforms and initiated the National Assessment of Educational Progress (NAEP), which keeps an ongoing record of school performance. While general participation is voluntary, all schools that receive Title I money must participate. This funding is set aside for low socio-economic and minority students, which includes a large percentage of ELLs.

Most recently, the **No Child Left Behind (NCLB)** act established requirements that school districts must meet to continue to receive federal funds. The law has a number of requirements, but the one that has affected ELLs most is the system of evaluating school performance based on disaggregated data. Schools can no longer rely on high-performing students to average out the low performance of language-challenged students. While the law is far from perfect, it prohibits schools from burying the low performance of any subpopulation in a school-wide average.

SKILL 7.2 Demonstrate knowledge of models and types of ESOL programs and of the characteristics, goals, and research on the effectiveness of various ESOL teaching approaches and methodologies

The major models of ESOL programs differ depending on the sources consulted. However, general consensus recognizes the following program models with different instructional methods used in the different programs.

Immersion Education Models
With these programs, instruction is initiated in the student's non-native language, using the second language as the medium of instruction for both academic content and the second language. Two of these models strive for full bilingualism: one is for language majority students and the other is for language minorities.

- **English Language Development (ELD) or English as a Second Language (ESL) Pull-out:** Pull-out programs include various approaches to teaching English to non-native speakers. In 1997, TESOL standards defined these approaches as marked by an intent to teach the ELL to communicate in social settings, engage in academic tasks, and use English in socially and culturally appropriate ways. Three well-known approaches to ELD or ESL are:

  - **Grammar-based ESL:** This method teaches <u>about</u> the language, stressing its structure, functions and vocabulary through rules, drills, and error correction.

  - **Communication-based ESL:** This approach emphasizes instruction in English that emphasizes <u>using</u> the language in meaningful contexts. There is little stress on correctness in the early stages and more emphasis on comprehensible input to foster communication and lower anxiety when risk-taking.

  - **Content-based ESL:** Instruction in English that attempts to develop language skills and prepare ELLs to study grade-level content material in English is content-based. There is emphasis on language, but with graded introduction to content areas, vocabulary and basic concepts.

- **Structured English immersion:** The goal is English proficiency. ELLs are pulled out for structured instruction in English so that subject matter is comprehensible. Used with sizeable groups of ELLs who speak the same language and are in the same grade level or with diverse populations of language minority students. There is little or no L1 language support. Teachers use sheltered instructional techniques and have strong receptive skills in the students' native or heritage language.

- **Submersion with primary language support:** The goal is English proficiency. Bilingual teachers or aides support the minority students in each grade level who are ELLs. In small groups, the ELLs are tutored by reviewing the content areas in their primary language. The teachers use the L1 to support English content classes; ELLs achieve limited literacy in L1.

- **Canadian French immersion (language-majority students):** The goal is bilingualism in French (L2) and English (L1). The targeted population is the language-majority. Students are immersed in the L2 for the first 2 years using sheltered language instruction, and then English L1 is introduced. The goal is all students of the majority language (English) becoming fluent in L2 (French).

- **Indigenous language immersion (endangered languages, such as Navajo):** The goal is bilingualism; the program is socially, linguistically and cognitively attuned to the native culture and community context. This approach supports endangered minority languages and develops academic skills in minority language and culture as well as in the English language and predominate culture.

SKILL 7.3   Demonstrate knowledge of current educational trends, issues, and policies in the field of ESOL and their relationships to program planning

Some of the issues of concern to educators are:

- increasing the length of the school day and year (U.S. students currently spend 180 days in school compared to Japan with 243, South Korea 220, Israel with 216, Luxembourg 216, and The Netherlands, Scotland and Thailand with 200.)
- improving student achievement
- Georgia school improvement program
- high-stakes testing
- improving Early Childhood Education
- improving teacher quality
- improving the retention rate of high school drop-outs
- making higher education affordable for everyone
- using educational technology in the classroom (*EvaluTech*) (www.evalutech.sreb.org)
- International Baccalaureate programs
- teaching technology in the classroom

SKILL 7.4   Demonstrate knowledge of strategies for pursuing professional growth opportunities in the field of ESOL (e.g., formulating a professional development plan, participating in professional associations and other academic organizations)

Professional development plans are guides to help teachers achieve their long term and short term goals as educators. By planning and writing down these goals, the teacher is more likely to achieve his or her goals than teachers who only keep these goals in their heads. A listing of goals, actions, and assessments will lead to a deeper understanding of the steps to be taken in achieving these goals and at the same time, promote personal reflection.

Participation in professional associations and other academic organizations provides the space for teaching professionals to connect to colleagues, receive new information about professional issues, learn about trends and research in the field, and be inspired with new ideas.

SKILL 7.5   Demonstrate knowledge of strategies for serving as a professional ESOL resource in the school community (e.g., modeling effective ESOL teaching practices, helping other teachers and school administrators to work effectively with ELL students, planning and implementing professional ESOL workshops for colleagues)

The ESOL professional is a resource person for the entire school community of educators who may be dubious when confronted with ELLs in their classroom. The ESOL professional can recommend good practices such as:

- always having a good supply of English learner dictionaries, bilingual dictionaries, picture dictionaries, alphabet letters (both print and cursive), art supplies, catalogues, magazines, games (including board games, card games, and computer games at appropriate age levels), realia, and other manipulatives.

In addition, the ESOL specialist may plan and implement workshops for colleagues that teach specific ESOL techniques and activities. Many, if not most, ESOL activities can be adapted to any level or age group.

Another duty of the ESOL resource person is to advocate for ELLs when cultural misunderstandings interfere with learning. She may also be requested to coordinate support and interagency support services for the ELLs.

SKILL 7.6 **Demonstrate knowledge of a variety of collaborative teaching models (e.g., parallel teaching, alternative teaching, team teaching) and ways to work with colleagues to assist ELL students as they transition into general education and content-area classrooms**

No one research-based teaching model has been shown to be more effective than another. The following examples show several models that are currently in use in the classroom.

- One teach, one observe: One teacher teaches the entire group while one observes and collects data on an individual student, a small group of students, or the entire class.
- One teach, one assist: One teacher instructs the entire group of students while the other professional is circulating among the students providing assistance.
- Parallel teaching: Two professionals split the group of students in half and simultaneously provide the same instruction.
- Station teaching: The teachers divide instruction into two, three, or even more nonsequential components, and each is addressed in a separate area of the room, with each student participating at each station in sequence.
- Alternative teaching: A teacher pulls a small group of students to the side of the room for instruction.
- Team teaching: Professionals who have built a strong collaborative relationship and have complementary teaching styles fluidly share the instructional responsibilities of the entire student group.

(Friend and Bursuck 2005 in Schumm, J.S. 2006)

COMPETENCY 8.0 **Understand how to serve as a resource liaison and advocate for ELL students and how to build effective partnerships with families and the community to support student learning and achievement**

SKILL 8.1 **Demonstrate knowledge of school and community resources available to ELL students and their families and apply knowledge of strategies for helping ELL students and their families participate fully in the school and community**

By advocating for the ELL student, the ESOL instructor can ensure that the students in his or her charge are able to participate in the school band, science club, math club, chess club, sports teams, and all other activities in which students of their age and inclination participate.

Encouraging students and their families to make full use of public resources such as the local public library, including its online facilities, will help students to expand their knowledge and understanding of help available to ELLs. In addition, many libraries have after school, Saturday, or holiday programs to encourage constructive use of students' time.

Museums, too, often have educational outreach programs that may be used by all citizens. Other resources such as parks and the local YMCA and YWCA or similar organizations offer recreational facilities to all citizens.

SKILL 8.2 **Demonstrate knowledge of ways to advocate for ELL students and their families in various school contexts, including how to support ELL students and their families in making decisions and advocating for themselves in the school community**

The State of Georgia has six different education models for the academic support of the ELL student:

1. Pull-out model outside the academic block – students are taken out of a non-academic class for the purpose of receiving small group language instruction.
2. Push-in model within the academic block – students remain in their general education class where they receive content instruction from their content area teacher and language assistance from the ESOL teacher.
3. A cluster center to which students are transported for instruction – students from two or more schools are grouped in a center designed to provide intensive language assistance.
4. A resource center / laboratory – students receive language assistance in a group setting supplemented by multi-media materials.
5. A scheduled class period – students at the middle and high school levels receive language assistance and /or content instruction in a class composed of ELLs only.

6. An alternative approved in advance by the Department of Education through a process described in Guidance accompanying this rule.

Where possible, it is to the advantage of the ESOL instructor to be prepared to explain and if necessary suggest alternatives to the families of ELLs, should educational challenges occur. Where parents are knowledgeable about their alternatives, they are better able to support their children and fully participate in the school community.

Caring teachers know that external factors can affect student behavior and performance in school. As advocates for students, including their health and safety, teachers must be alert to issues such as eating disorders, emotional distress, suicidal tendencies, substance abuse, and child abuse or neglect which can affect performance and even students' lives. While it is not the teacher's role to resolve these issues, it is a moral and legal obligation to report suspected cases of abuse to the "person in charge". Timely intervention can be the key to a better existence.

SKILL 8.3 Demonstrate knowledge of strategies for working with colleagues to provide comprehensive, challenging educational opportunities for ELL students and for ensuring ELL students' full access to school resources, including educational technology

Team teaching, parallel teaching, alternative teaching, etc. with colleagues from other educational specialties, perspectives and backgrounds are exciting opportunities to be taken advantage of. They can provide the framework for successful teaching of ELL students and ensuring that these students reach their full potential. One of the most difficult problems for co-teachers is the lack of time to thoroughly plan the lessons. Teachers need to clearly define their individual roles and agree to be flexible when undertaking collaborative efforts.

While ELLs are guaranteed full access to all school resources including technology, they have special needs that can be enhanced by special software programs. The use of translation programs to support learning, especially for those groups of ELLs where there is no native language resource person, can be helpful to those ELLs who are having difficulty in grasping concepts or understanding vocabulary. Several software translation programs are available that can help with this problem:

- Babel Fish (http://world.altavista.com)
- Free Translator (http://www.free-translator.com)
- World Lingo (http://www.worldlingo.com)

SKILL 8.4 **Identify the benefits of, and strategies for, creating effective partnerships between the school and various community resources to support ELL students' learning and achievement**

When the ESOL teacher is able to point out resources and community members who "have made it", motivation to succeed is increased.

One of the most promising pieces of legislation to support ELL students' learning and achievement is the proposed "DREAM Act" (The Development, Relief and Education Alien Minors Act.) The Dream Act is a proposed piece of federal legislation introduced in the U.S. Congress on March 26, 2009. This legislation provides the opportunity to minor aliens to earn conditional permanent residency if they graduate from U.S. high schools, are of good moral character, and have been in the country continuously for five years or more prior to the bill's enactment.

Various community organizations provide scholarships to children of different heritages for the advancement of their education. One website portal (http://www.scholarshipsforhispanics.com/) lists possible contacts for Hispanics searching for scholarships.

SKILL 8.5 **Recognize the important roles that families play in their children's development and demonstrate knowledge of culturally responsive strategies for communicating and building partnerships with ELL students' families**

Often in schools, parents, grandparents, and other people involved in children's lives want to take a more active role in the educational process. They also all seem to have an opinion on the appropriate method for teaching students how to read. Sometimes this can lead to controversy and misunderstandings.

It is important to provide opportunities for the public to come into the school and participate in activities designed to encourage their participation in the schooling of their children. During these fun programs, it is just as important to share tidbits of information about the methodologies and strategies being implemented. In this way, the public can begin to understand the differences in ESOL instruction today in comparison to what it may have been in their native cultures when they attended school. This comparison addresses what is often the biggest statement of concern made by adults concerning current educational trends.

Taking the time to educate parents and other family members not only helps to enhance understanding and open communication, it can also provide more support for students than the school alone would ever be able to provide.

Some strategies for educating parents and family members include:

- Bingo games where the correct answer on the Bingo board is a fact about English language instruction
- small parent workshops offered on various topics
- newsletter pieces or paragraphs
- individual parent meetings
- inviting parents to observe lessons
- small pieces of information shared during other social times where parents are invited into the school

Communicating general information about English and appropriate English language instruction is important. It is just as important to share specific information about students with parents, other school personnel, and the community. Once the teacher has gathered sufficient information on the students, he/she must find appropriate methods to share this information with those who need the data. Again, depending on the audience, the amount and type of information shared may vary. Some ways to share information with parents/guardians include:

- individual parent meetings
- small group meetings
- regular parent updates through phone calls
- charts and graphs of progress sent home
- notes home

SKILL 8.6 **Demonstrate knowledge of strategies for establishing an educational environment that supports, develops, and encourages the social, academic, and political involvement of ELL students' families in the school community**

Parents and other family members often delight in being part of the educational community when encouraged to do so. Schools which encourage all the stakeholders in the community to participate in the school system have strong community resources upon which to draw when (and if) problems occur.

Through outreach programs:

- older members of the community can be encouraged to mentor at-risk students.
- parents and grandparents can serve as tutors for students with academic difficulties.
- room mothers and fathers provide support for the many classroom events throughout the school year.
- the PTA groups are an excellent place for family members with organizational and financial skills to serve the school community.
- Invitations to relatives of ELL students to talk about their homelands and cultures are an excellent way to encourage otherwise reticent parents to get involved in their school.

SUBAREA 3.0   ESOL PLANNING, IMPLEMENTATION, AND
                     ASSESSMENT

COMPETENCY 9.0   Understand standards-based ESOL curriculum planning
                     and implementation.

SKILL 9.1   Recognize how to plan ESOL instruction around standards-based subject matter and language-learning objectives

Content-based instruction (CBI) or "Sheltered Instruction" integrates L2 acquisition and the basic content areas of math, science, social studies, literature, etc. The most current research continues to find validity in the following:

- Learners do not learn L2 through singular instruction in the language's rules; they learn from meaningful interaction in the language.
- Learners will gain proficiency in a language, only if they receive adequate input, i.e., speaking and listening start to make sense to a learner when they can build upon previous knowledge as well as understand context and cues.
- Although conversational fluency in L2 is a goal, speaking is not sufficient to develop the academic cognitive skills needed to learn the basic content areas.

The goal in every classroom is for English Language Learners (ELLs) to achieve the standards in basic content areas (math, science, social studies, etc.). To accomplish this goal, ELLs must learn "academic language" which takes from five to seven years, according to Cummins (1993-2003). TESOL standards relating to academics state that the students will:

- use English to interact in the classroom.
- use English to obtain, process construct, and provide subject matter information in spoken and written form.
- use appropriate learning strategies to construct and apply academic knowledge.

Because ELLs typically encounter issues with vocabulary when being instructed in the content areas, vocabulary needs to be pre-taught and reinforced frequently to ensure the achievement of the academic language Cummins mentions.

SKILL 9.2   Demonstrate knowledge of current instructional approaches, methods, and instructional practices in the field of ESOL

There is no one method or strategy that is effective in all situations or with all ELLs. Thinking today suggests an eclectic approach, using elements from many different methods and strategies to ensure ELLs get the most access to the language arts curriculum and to learning.

Total Physical Response is a systematized approach using commands devised by psychologist James Asher (1982). TPR is an effective means of introducing students and adults to a second language. It works on listening skills in the early developmental stage or with students who have had no previous exposure to English. Teachers speak a command, e.g. "Stand up" and the students respond physically. The teacher continues with other commands until the activity reaches its end. There is no pressure to speak, so the affective filter is lowered. This is especially useful with beginners who may be in a "silent period".

The Natural Approach, devised by Krashen and Terrell (1983), exposes children to new vocabulary used in meaningful context. Students receive extended listening experiences including TPR, colorful pictures explaining concepts, and active involvement through physical contact with the pictures and objects being discussed. They make choices, answer yes-no questions, and engage in game-like situations. For listening comprehension, ELLs conduct meaningful communication and acquire language instead of learning it.

The Cognitive Academic Language Learning Approach (CALLA) (Chamot & O'Malley, 1994) assists in the transition from an ESOL-driven language arts program to a "mainstream" language arts program by teaching ELLs how to handle content area material with success. CALLA helps intermediate and advanced students understand and retain content area material while they are improving their English language skills. CALLA lessons incorporate content-area lessons based on the grade-level curriculum in science, math, social studies, etc. The language functions used in the content class such as describing, classifying, explaining, etc. must be acquired by the student. Learning strategy instruction will be given to foster critical and creative thinking skills so that ELLs develop the ability to solve problems, extrapolate, make inferences, etc.

The **Whole Language Approach** increases linguistic, cognitive and early literacy skills in an integrated fashion by developing all four language skills (listening, speaking, writing, and reading) (Goodman, Goodman, & Hood, 1989). This approach incorporates elements from several instructional strategies to further reading and writing skills. The primary strategy is the Language Experience Approach.

Activating Background Knowledge is essential for material to be meaningful. Material is not meaningful unless it is related to existing knowledge that the learner possesses (Omaggio, 1993). Otherwise, schemas are not activated and the material remains free of meaning according to the Schema Theory of Carrell and Eisterhold (1983). Teachers must include activities in their lesson plans to activate students' previous knowledge on topics being presented.

Storytelling provides natural language experiences for all levels of learners. Stories for the classroom should be easily understood or familiar to the students from their native cultures. Stories using repetitive patterns are desirable for their language. The story should lend itself to dramatization and pantomime to encourage theater and mime activities.

SKILL 9.3 **Recognize the importance of planning ESOL instruction based on assessment of ELL students' language proficiency and prior knowledge**

There are a myriad of tests for determining the placement of language students. Formal assessment can be divided into before, during and after course tests. Before course tests are usually aptitude tests. During a course, the ELLs may be tested by placement tests, diagnostic tests, progress tests, and achievement tests. After completing a course, students are typically tested by proficiency tests. In a school setting, these tests may be in a student's records from previous years or new testing may need to be done.

In order to determine appropriate instruction, teachers need accurate information from the appropriate tests. **Placement tests** can either be based on a theory of language proficiency or on the learning objectives of the class or course. They are often easy to administer and to grade, though not particularly reliable. This is not a primary concern as ELLs can be moved between levels as appropriate.

Diagnostic tests are used to determine an ELLs' areas of strength and weakness so that appropriate types and levels of teaching and learning tasks are given.

Cummins (1981) observed that the academic language of the content areas prevents many ELLs from achieving success in school so **instruction in the native or heritage language** may be an appropriate option for beginning English language learners. Krashen and Biber (1988) believed that comprehensible input is a critical element in effective instruction in English. However, by combining content instruction with English as the medium of instruction, ELLs can learn impressive amounts of English as well as their content materials.

When using English and the heritage (native) language to deliver content, instructors should remember:

- ELLs who speak a different language from English have varying abilities and talents just as English speaking children do.
- Content area instruction must be delivered using sound instructional methods that promote both formal and informal registers in the heritage language as well as in English.
- When permitted to develop their heritage language in positive ways, ELLS become positive members of society who will benefit from the ability to function in two languages all their lives.
- ELLs are capable of speaking, reading, and writing English at the same level as their English-speaking peers.
- Better employment opportunities are available for bilinguals than monolinguals, so ELLs should actively develop language literacy in both languages.

SKILL 9.4   Demonstrate knowledge of strategies for addressing ELL students' varying educational backgrounds (e.g., limited formal schooling) and varying levels of English language proficiency when planning and delivering standards-based instruction

For beginning students, Total Physical Response by Asher (1982) allows LEPs to participate without forcing speech in the beginning of their introduction to the English language. TPR consists of the instructor issuing commands which are carried out by the students. The popular children's game 'Simon Says' can be used after the vocabulary items have been introduced in the classroom for a slightly different way to achieve the same goals.

Krashen and Terrell (1983) developed the Natural Approach. Students are introduced to new vocabulary by different experiences. Through listening experiences, TPR, vividly colored pictures that illustrate concepts and active involvement with the pictures, learners are able to make choices, answer yes-no questions, and play games.

The Cognitive Academic Language Learning Approach (CALLA) launched by Chamot and O'Malley (1994) helps intermediate and advanced students understand and retain content area material as they are enhancing their English language skills. CALLA helps ELLs by giving instruction in the appropriate language arts (specialized vocabulary, syntax, phonology) while dealing with the different content areas. Learning strategies that emphasize critical and creative thinking skills such as problem solving, inferencing, etc., need to be taught during these lessons, since they are critical to success in the mainstream classroom.

The Whole Language Approach of Goodman, Goodman and Hood (1989) stresses the importance of developing all four language skills through an integrated approach. The Language Experience Approach is one of many different instructional strategies used to achieve this goal. Children dictate their own stories based on a shared experience and then practice "reading" it until a firm grasp of the story is achieved.

ELLs must have background knowledge before they are able to succeed in content classrooms. Frequently, they are unable to relate to the present experience because they are unfamiliar with the topic at hand, but if appropriate experiences are presented, ELLs are better able to deal with the situation. In order to activate the background schema, Carrell and Eisterhold (1983) stress the importance of teachers activating prior knowledge in order for ELLs to succeed in content classrooms. Background knowledge is activated through eliciting shared information from students before introducing new or similar topics.

Storytelling is another way of increasing language experiences for ELLs, even during very early stages of language acquisition. Wajnryb (1986) claimed that storytelling has many benefits because:

- it is genuine communication.
- it is an oral tradition meant to be heard.
- it is real.
- it is sensual.
- it appeals to the affective domain.
- it is appreciated by the individual while at the same time creating a sense of community.
- it reduces anxiety by forging a listening experience.
- it is pedagogically positive.

By introducing these ESOL techniques, the curriculum is adjusted without isolating the ELLs from mainstream work.

SKILL 9.5   Demonstrate knowledge of strategies for creating a secure, positive, and motivating language-learning environment for ELL students that encourages them to be actively involved in learning, to take risks, and to extend their learning inside and outside the classroom

In order for language minority students to learn English and meet the National Educational Goals, a secure, positive and motivating language-learning environment must be provided. How schools meet these criteria depends on the individual school and its district.

A positive learning environment is acquired when the school presents a safe and attractive environment free of prejudices. The school should also be one where administrators and instructors exact high expectations for linguistically and culturally appropriate learning experiences from the student body. The teachers, administrators and other staff should be trained to prepare instructional materials and other services specifically for language minority students.

The school should be a place where is the input of language minority parents is welcomed, as they are the at-home primary teachers of their children. Parents should be informed of decisions affecting their children, their schools and school districts. **(Adapted from TESOL: ESL Standards for Pre-K—12 Students.)**

Strategies for providing a safe and secure environment may include assigning a "buddy" from the same country or language group to go with the newcomer during the day and show him or her such essential things as where the bathroom and cafeteria are, how to line up and receive food in the cafeteria, and how to eat specific foods given out in the cafeteria.

Another way is to follow predictable routines in the classroom. Predictability is important for all students, but especially ELLs and those whose lives may have been in turmoil for some time.

Placing new students in the center or front section of the classroom is a way to integrate them into the mainstream of activities even if they do not speak a word of English. If groups are used in the classroom, the new ELLs should be placed in a group that remains stable for a long period of time to establish a mini community of interdependence.

SKILL 9.6   **Recognize how to incorporate a variety of activities in instruction that develops authentic uses of language and explores content-area topics in order to maximize ELL students' language learning and concept development**

Language study using authentic language and the uses of language have become the watchwords in language acquisition. Theorists now believe that language use is the proper goal of language studies and that language should be studied in context instead of in isolated sentences which only provide examples of a specific grammar point or structure. In the move away from de-contextualized, graded textbooks, researchers encourage the study of discourse above the sentence level.

Teachers need to provide a wide range of materials, including educational technology (cassettes, video, computers, and CD-ROMs), to create a language-rich environment, which is believed to be the key to comprehensible input and high motivation.

And finally, all the four language skills—listening, speaking, reading and writing – should be practiced at all levels. One way of achieving the practice of all four skills while using authentic language is to incorporate task-based activities into the instruction (1985). Here we define a task as "an activity or action which is carried out as a result of processing or understanding language,"

SKILL 9.7   **Demonstrate knowledge of how to scaffold oral and written language tasks in order to facilitate ELL students' achievement of academic tasks and to promote their language development and learning**

Scaffolding, or supporting, children of all ages consists of demonstrating, guiding, and teaching in a step-by-step process while ELLs are trying to communicate effectively and develop their language skills (Cazden 1983; Ninio & Bruner 1976). The amount of scaffolding depends on the support needed and the individual child. It allows the ELL to assume more and more responsibility as he or she is able. Once the ELLs feel secure in their abilities, they are ready to move on to the next stage.

Educational scaffolding consists of several linked strategies, including modeling academic language and contextualizing academic language using visuals, gestures, and demonstrations to help students while they are involved in hands-on learning. Some efficient scaffolding techniques are: providing direction, clarifying purpose, keeping the student on task with proposed rubrics that clarify expectations, offering suggestions for resources, and supplying lessons or activities without problems.

Tompkins (2006) identified five levels of scaffolding for learning and problem solving to show how ELLs moved from needing considerable support to the independent level where they are ready to solve problems on their own.

- **Modeling**: The instructor models orally or through written supports (a paragraph, a paper, an example) the work expected of the ELL. Projects from previous years can provide examples of the type of work expected.
- **Shared:** ELLs use their pooled knowledge of the project (and that of their teacher) to complete the assignment.
- **Interactive:** The teacher allows ELLs to question her on points that need clarification or are not understood, i.e. everyone is a learner. It is especially satisfying for the student when the teacher admits that she does not know the answer and helps the students locate it.
- **Guided:** Well-posed questions, clues, reminders and examples are all ways of guiding the ELL towards the goal.
- **Independent levels:** The learner achieves independence and no longer needs educational scaffolding.

SKILL 9.8 Recognize how to create learning opportunities that integrate comprehension through listening, speaking, reading, writing, and viewing for a variety of academic and social purposes

Second language teaching (SLT) recognizes the importance of giving ELLs assignments which further their language goals by engaging them in integrative tasks which include any or all of the following language skills: listening, speaking, reading, writing, and viewing. A task are loosely defined as any activity which emphasizes meaning over form. Which tasks are chosen depends on the teacher, who makes decisions about appropriate tasks for her classroom.

Candlin (1987, in Batstone 1994: 17) suggests that good tasks are those which:

- encourage learners to attend to meaning
- give learners flexibility in problem solving
- involve learners whose personality and attitude is primary
- are challenging, but not too demanding
- raise ELLs' awareness of the process of language use, encouraging them to reflect on their own language use

Tasks can be divided into two different types. Learning tasks are those which focus on formal features of language and have specific learning outcomes. Communicative tasks are typically focused on meaning and are frequently open-ended. Often they are used in group work and may have a written component which summarizes the work.

Tasks may be divided into three main groups:

- **Information-gap tasks** involve the transfer of given information from one person to another, from one form to another, or from one place to another. The activity often involves selection of relevant information as well, and learners may have to meet criteria of completeness and correctness in making the transfer.
- **Reasoning-gap tasks** involve deriving some new information from given information through processes of inference, deduction, practical reasoning, or a perception of relationships or patterns.
- **Opinion-gap tasks** involve identifying and articulating a personal preference, feeling or attitude in response to a given situation.
  (Adapted from Prabhu 1987: 46-47)

Authenticity is an important component of tasks in the classroom. Many instructors and researchers believe that learning tasks should be authentic, using "real" spoken English. However, Nunan (1989) suggests that the distinction between real world tasks and pedagogic tasks may be blurred. He believes that pedagogic activities, while they may seem artificial, may in fact be practicing enabling skills such as fluency, discourse and interactional skills, mastery of phonological elements, and mastery of grammar. He suggests that the distinction between real-world and pedagogic tasks may be more of a continuum than a hard and fast distinction.

COMPETENCY 10.0   **Understand how to locate, develop, adapt, and use resources effectively in ESOL instruction, including technological resources.**

SKILL 10.1   **Recognize how to locate, develop, adapt, and use an appropriate variety of materials and resources to promote ELL students' language, literacy, and content-area development, including books and other print materials, visual aids, props, games, realia, and technology**

The text itself is a resource that may or may not increase comprehension, depending on how it is written. In general, texts which have long sentences and more advanced words are more complex than texts with short, simple sentence structures and basic vocabulary words. For ELLs, it may be necessary to obtain basic readers to help them overcome these difficulties.

Sometimes texts are complicated and difficult to understand because they discuss topics not familiar to the reader. When the student's prior knowledge or background knowledge is activated, the ELL is able to attach meaning to new information by joining the new with the old to achieve comprehension. Children who come from backgrounds where reading was not possible or who did not attend a pre-school program may be at a disadvantage when entering a mainstream kindergarten or school reading program.

Texts may be difficult for beginning readers because they are not user-friendly. Texts which highlight new vocabulary, summarize key points, and contain introductions and summaries include features that will help the struggling reader.

According to Vygotsky (1978), the sociocultural context from which a student comes is crucial. The community, home, school, and classroom contexts exert influence on the performance of an individual student or a group of students. Students who have been classified as low achievers in reading may resent the stigma and continue to perform poorly or react negatively to assessment.

Atkinson & Hansen (1966-1967) published the first study of the use of computers in reading instruction. Students at Stanford University accessed reading lessons similar to traditional worksheets on a mainframe computer. Today, the computer is used in all aspects of our lives, and today's students, with one computer for every five students, will experience some form of computer learning.

Blanton & Menendez (2006 in Schumm, ed., *Reading Assessment and Instruction for All Learners*) mention seven categories discussing how computers are used in reading instruction:

- **Game applications,** such as Reader Rabbit, Missing Link, and Reading Blaster
- **General applications,** such as Microsoft Word, PowerPoint, Hyperstudio, Kid Pix, and Story Book Weaver
- **Access applications**, such as Google, Netscape, and Yahooligans
- **Tutoring applications,** such as Watch Me Read
- **Thinking and problem-solving applications,** such as Oregon Trail, SimCity, SimEarth, and Zoombinis Island Odyssey
- **Communication applications,** such as email and online discussion spaces
- **Integrated learning systems (ILSs),** such as the Waterford Early Reading Program, Fast ForWord, and Read 180

Other resources include **graphic organizers** which help students visualize raw data. These can be used by the teacher for simplification of complex materials, numerous data, or complicated relationships in content areas. Students learn to analyze data, organize information, and clarify concepts. Examples are: pie charts, flow charts, bar diagrams, Venn diagrams, family trees, spider maps, organizational charts, and strip maps.

Still other graphic organizers are webbing, concept mapping, passwords and language ladders, and brainstorming.

- With **webbing**, students learn to associate words or phrases with a topic or concept.
- By using **concept maps**, students learn the relationships between the different elements of a topic and how to organize them from the most general to the most specific. This is different from webbing where relationships between words or phrases are shown, but not ranked.
- **Passwords and language ladders** are motivating ways to teach chunks of language to ELLs. The "password" of the day is language needed for daily student life in school. After the words or phrases are explained, they are posted on the board, and must be used before leaving the room or participating in some activity. Language ladders are associated words such as different ways to say hello or good-bye.
- **Brainstorming** consists of students contributing ideas related to a concept or problem-centered topic. The teacher initially accepts all ideas without comment. Students then categorize, prioritize, and select proposed selections for further investigation.

SKILL 10.2 **Demonstrate knowledge of strategies for selecting and adapting materials and other resources in the ESOL classroom in order to ensure that instructional resources are appropriate to ELL students' developing language and content-area skills and abilities**

Scaffolding, or supporting, children of all ages consists of demonstrating, guiding, and teaching in a step-by-step process while ELLs are trying to communicate effectively and develop their language skills (Cazden 1983; Ninio & Bruner 1976). The amount of scaffolding depends on the support needed and the individual child. It allows the ELL to assume more and more responsibility as he or she is able. Once the ELLs feel secure in their abilities, they are ready to move on to the next stage.

Educational scaffolding consists of several linked strategies including modeling academic language and contextualizing academic language using visuals, gestures, and demonstrations to help students while they are involved in hands-on learning. Some efficient scaffolding techniques are: providing direction, clarifying purpose, keeping the student on task with proposed rubrics that clarify expectations, offering suggestions for resources, and supplying lessons or activities without problems.

Tompkins (2006) identified five levels of scaffolding for learning and problem solving to show how ELLs moved from needing considerable support to the independent level where they are ready to solve problems on their own.

- **Modeling**: The instructor models orally or through written supports (a paragraph, a paper, an example) the work expected of the ELL. Projects from previous years can provide examples of the type of work expected.
- **Shared:** ELLs use their pooled knowledge of the project (and that of their teacher) to complete the assignment.
- **Interactive:** The teacher allows ELLs to question her on points that need clarification or are not understood, i.e. everyone is a learner. It is especially satisfying for the student when the teacher admits that she does not know the answer and helps the students locate it.
- **Guided:** Well-posed questions, clues, reminders and examples are all ways of guiding the ELL towards the goal.
- **Independent levels:** The learner achieves independence and no longer needs educational scaffolding.

Scaffolding is not the only way to adapt materials for ELLs. Other techniques such as using facial expressions and gestures help ELLs understand materials that may be at their instruction level (what Krashen calls *i* + 1), i.e. just above their level of understanding. Both of these techniques can be overused and limit student learning if the ELLs are not sufficiently challenged academically.

Teachers make the material comprehensible to the students when they guide the ELLs through the story or other text so that it is connected to their lives in a meaningful way.

Questions such as, "What can we learn from this?", "How can we do this in real life?", "How are people like this?" etc. are part of the teacher's repertoire, but are especially important when dealing with ELLs who may not be able to see how this activity relates to their lives and incorporate the message or meaning of the text or other material unless led by clever questions. For history, questions would include "Why?", "Where?", What happened?," and summarizing by "Therefore." Other content areas have their own vocabulary and other language conventions, and teachers must teach for the ELLs to become successful in their content areas.

Another excellent technique to cement ELLs' learning is to teach the different ways of using mapping or graphic organizers so that students learn to analyze the materials presented to them in a way that helps to visualize the main points and their connections.

SKILL 10.3 Recognize how to select, adapt, and use culturally responsive, age-appropriate and linguistically accessible materials to promote ELL students' language, literacy, and content-area development, including appropriate use of primary-language materials

Language-rich environments are crucial when dealing with ELLs in the classroom. No two people learn alike, so diverse materials on the same subject may help the student bridge the gap between prior knowledge and knowledge to be acquired.

Students with little or no English or previous educational experience may be taught in their native language when possible. Research shows that, contrary to previous beliefs, students who are taught content in their native or heritage language are able to receive simultaneous language instruction in English to their benefit (Slavin and Cheung, 2003).

For those students who have reached a certain level of competency in English, scaffolding is recommended. ELL students need extra help with vocabulary, linguistic complexities, idioms, prefixes and suffixes, and false cognates. (Teachers who are able can easily increase ELLs' vocabulary using cognate instruction).

For further suggestions, teachers may research their specific needs in the data banks of the following organizations:

Organizations providing additional resources to educators of ELLs:

- **Teachers of English to Speakers of Other Languages** and its regional affiliates
  www.tesol.org

- **Georgia Teachers of English to Speakers of Other Languages**
  www.gatesol.org

- **Center for Applied Linguistics**
  www.cal.org

- **U.S. Department of Education's Office of English Language Acquisition Language Enhancement, and Academic Achievement for Limited English Proficient Students (OELA)**
  www.ed.gov/offices/OELA/

Books and journals offer supplemental resources for addressing cultural, ethnic and linguistic differences. Among the noteworthy are:

- **Beebe, Von N. and Mackey, William F. Bilingual Schooling and the Miami Experience.** Coral Gables: Institute of Inter-American Studies. Graduate School of International Studies. University of Miami, 1990. Extensively documents the influx of Cuban refugees into the Miami-Dade County school system.

- **TESOL Journal**

- **Bilingual Research Journal**

Several websites provide additional resources for teachers of ELLs:
English Language Learner Knowledge Base
www.helpforschools.com/ELLKBase/index.shtml

- Valuable for the latest information on ELLS, including conferences, program evaluations, legislation, parental outreach, and a data base. Also see: SOLOM at www.helpforschools.com/ELLKBase/forms/SOLOM.shtml

WebQuests
http://webquest.sdsu.edu

- WebQuests support teachers with a scaffold for organizing theme-based research units by using the Internet as a learning tool and source of information.

Wiggle Works
www.ed.gov/pubs/TechStrength/scholastic.html

- This early literacy, bilingual series incorporates universally designed CD-ROMs for each book in the database. (from Scholastic and the Center for Applied Special Technology)

N.B. The resources listed above are concerned not only with learning, but in many cases deal with the socio-linguistic areas of culture, also.

SKILL 10.4 Demonstrate knowledge of strategies for helping ELL students select and use a variety of resources for different social and academic purposes (e.g., research, independent reading)

ELLs will probably have to be taught how to use resource materials for research just like their native speaking counterparts. As students begin a project, they may fill in a KWL strategy chart. The chart is organized in three columns and each student (or group) fills it in appropriately for their project/paper:

- List what you know
- List what you want to know
- List what you learned

Based on the information obtained, the student can be guided to the appropriate research materials in the library or on the Internet. A tour of the library or media center at the beginning of the school year is an excellent way to introduce the library or refresh the memory of those who are familiar with it. Skilled librarians can help students pinpoint the information they need while at the same time suggesting other sources for further investigation.

When introducing students to independent reading, one of the best strategies is to find books on a subject the student likes. For boys, this is frequently sports and for girls, romances. However, this is a generalization and observation of the student can lead to other books or authors which will interest the student.

SKILL 10.5 Demonstrate knowledge of strategies for evaluating and using appropriate multimedia and technological resources to enhance language, literacy, and content-area instruction for ELL students (e.g., computers and related devices, software, the Internet)

Roblyer (2006) in *Integrating Education Technology into Teaching* suggests that there are two types of criteria that should be considered when evaluating software for classroom instruction. The first type includes essential criteria and the second type is optional or situational – characteristics which are applied dependent upon the user's needs.

The **first type** of software evaluation includes **four sets of essential criteria** categorized as follows:

Set 1: Essential instructional design and pedagogy characteristics: Does it teach?

- appropriate teaching strategy, based on best known methods
- presentation on screen contains nothing that misleads or confuses students
- comments to students not abusive or insulting
- readability at an appropriate level for students who will use it
- graphics fulfill important purpose and are not distracting to learners
- criteria specific to software types

Set 2: Essential content characteristics: Is content accurate, current, and appropriate?

- no grammar, spelling or punctuation errors on the screen
- all content accurate and up to date
- no racial or gender stereotypes: not geared toward only one sex or to certain races
- social characteristics are appropriate
- match to instructional needs

Set 3: Essential user interface characteristics: Is it "user friendly" and easy to navigate?

- User has appropriate control of movement within the program.
- User can turn off sound, if desired.
- Interface is intuitive.

Set 4: Essential technical soundness characteristics: Does it work correctly?

- Program loads consistently, without error.
- Program does not break, no matter what the student enters.
- Program works on desired platform.
- Program does what the screen says it should do.
- Online links work correctly.
- Videos and animations work correctly.

The **second type** of criteria focus on instructional design, interface/navigation, teacher use, presentation, technical and publisher support. These points should be used to judge between programs should they all possess the essential criteria.

The **Internet** is a tool and as such should be used with an instructional purpose in mind. Instructors should ask themselves if the Internet is the most efficient and effective medium to reach the instructional goals. The following guidelines will help in the determining the value of such projects.

- Projects should be meaningful, well-designed and interesting to the students.
- The Internet is a tool and not an end in itself.
- Projects should have specific goals and be timely.
- Start small until you gain experience in planning telecommunications projects.
- Communicate frequently (at least once a week) with all participants.
- Share the results of the project with the participants, the school and the community.

Two valuable resources for ESOL teachers are WebQuests and electronic portfolios. By using these tools, teachers are able to create their own projects based on established criteria.

- **WebQuests** were developed by Bernie Dodge of San Diego State University. They allow students to work independently or in small groups while doing research, problem solving, and application of basic skills. The essential components of WebQuests are Introduction, Task, Process, Resources, Evaluation, and Conclusion.

- **An electronic portfolio** is a concise, annotated collection of a student's work that displays his/her knowledge, understanding, skills, accomplishments, interests, and achievements over a period of time. By placing this information on the Web or a CD-Rom, the student is able to communicate with teachers, parents and others about their learning. The key elements of an electronic portfolio are: deciding on goals; designing flow charts, storyboards, and templates needed for the portfolio; developing the multimedia elements needed; creating the portfolio; and evaluating the product and the process.

COMPETENCY 11.0 **Understand current concepts, trends, issues, policies, and practices related to assessing ELL students, including different types of assessments used in ESOL programs and their purposes, uses, and limitations.**

SKILL 11.1 **Recognize the importance of using a variety of different assessment strategies with ELL students (e.g., observation, portfolio, student self-assessment, formal assessment)**

The following are examples of alternative assessments which offer options for an instructor.

Portfolios:
Portfolios are a collection of the student's work over a period of time (report cards, creative writing and drawing, etc.) that also function as assessments, because they:

- *indicate a range of competencies and skills*
- *are representative of instructional goals and academic growth*

Conferencing:
This assessment tool allows the instructor to evaluate a student's progress or decline. Students also learn techniques for self-evaluation.

Oral Interviews:
Teachers can use oral interviews to evaluate the language the students are using or their ability to provide content information when asked questions—both of which have implications for further instructional planning.

Teacher Observation:
During this type of assessment, the instructor observes the student behavior during an activity alone or within a group. Before the observation occurs, the instructor may want to create a numerical scale to rate desired outcomes.

Documentation:
Documentation shares similarities with teacher observations. However, documentation tends to transpire over a period of time, rather than isolated observations.

Interviews:
This type of assessment allows instructors to evaluate the student's level of English proficiency, as well as to identify potential problem areas, which may require correctional strategies.

Self-Assessment:
Students benefit tremendously from a self-assessment, because through the process of self-analysis they begin to think for themselves. Instructors need to provide guidance as well as the criteria related to success.

Student Journals:
Students benefit from journals because they are useful for keeping records, as well as for promoting an inner dialogue.

Story or Text Retelling:
Students respond orally and can be assessed on how well they describe events in the story or text as well as their response to the story.

Experiments and/or Demonstrations:
Students complete an experiment or demonstration and present it through an oral or written report. Students can be evaluated on their understanding of the concept, explanation of the scientific method, and /or their language proficiency.

Constructed Response Items:
Students respond in writing to open-ended questions. This method focuses on how students apply information rather than on how much they recall of content lessons. In this assessment, they may use a semantic map, a brief comment on a couple of points made in the readings, or an essay discussing or evaluating the material.

SKILL 11.2 Recognize the importance of, and strategies for, aligning assessment with curriculum and instruction

A basic premise of assessment is "test what you teach." In the high-stakes testing of today, teachers are expected to show good results with the exit tests of their students. Therefore, teachers can use regular classroom testing to determine and monitor each individual student's strengths and weaknesses. By aligning instruction of the ELLs with the curriculum, the instructor can plan reinforcement of the deficit skills as needed. This is effective in preventing later gaps when more complex skills are introduced. By integrating language skills into the content area at all times, the instructor can make the language classroom a motivating place with many opportunities for further learning.

In the case of students demonstrating possible learning difficulties, the classroom teacher will have the preliminary diagnostics with which to recommend further testing.

SKILL 11.3 Demonstrate knowledge of the challenges associated with assessment of ELL students and demonstrate awareness of psychological issues (e.g., test anxiety, limited testing experiences) and issues related to cultural and linguistic bias (e.g., unfamiliar images or references, unfamiliar test language or formats) that may affect ELL students' assessment results

Instructors of ELL students need to be aware of the less obvious cultural and linguistic bias in tests, such as students who are unfamiliar with the test-taking techniques of multiple-choice questions and/or bubble answer sheets.

The debate as to the unfairness and/or cultural bias often associated with the practice of standardized tests for assessment seems to be particularly true in the case of ELL learners. It has been argued by some that the "very use of tests is unfair, because tests are used to deprive people of color of their place in society" (Díaz-Rico & Weed, 1995.) However, the use of such testing as an assessment tool for ELL learners is standard and will continue to be so in the foreseeable future. That being said, the following factors can affect how a test or assessment is administered to the ELL learner and should be taken into consideration:

Anxiety:
Testing for an ELL may go well beyond what is considered "normal" anxiety for an native English speaker. ELLs are potentially at a much greater disadvantage, because not only is there anxiety about studying for a test, but also the test format itself could be unfamiliar, depending on the ELL's culture and previous test-taking experience. Multiple choice questions and especially "cloze" or fill-in-the-blanks, can be intimidating. Such formats may not be a true indicator of the ELL's actual level of ELL proficiency (Díaz-Rico & Weed, 1995.) A potential "workaround" to reduce the ELL's anxiety would be to administer practice tests to allow the ELL to develop a comfort level.

Time Limitations:
The time limitations, to which L1 learners in the U.S. are typically very accustomed, may create issues for ELLs of other cultures, especially in Europe. In the U.S., it is customary for the instructor to assign a class period to complete an exam, or for L1 learners to take statewide school achievement tests, which are timed in a non-negotiable fashion and do not allow the learner to skip forward or back. ELLs may need additional time, depending on their comfort level and experience.

Instructor/Learner rapport:
If the ELL does not share a comfortable relationship with the instructor, and/or there are significant language barriers between them, the ELL may not be forthcoming about any questions or clarification needed about the test. Without the ability or comfort level to address these issues, the ELL's success could be compromised before the test even begins. Furthermore, nuances of the English language, idiomatic phrasing, and confusing instructions can also negatively impact the ELL's test performance.

Troublesome Testing Content:

Achievement tests for measuring abilities other than language may contain cultural biases or incorrect translations, which can compromise the scoring for the ELL learner. For example, some words tend to be lost in translation, such as the word "belfry" in English and its corresponding word in Spanish, which is "campanario." "Belfry" is not common in everyday language use, but is usually found in classic literature. However, "campanario" is commonly used in Spanish. The ELL learner's overall achievement on such a test could be greatly diminished by unequal translation.

In addition to the above mentioned factors, cultural and linguistic bias often occurs in tests in other ways. For example, the story in the English culture generally has a hero and a villain. The leading character is pro-active, assertive, and in search of a goal for which he or she will be rewarded (a pot of gold, the charming prince, or a safe haven). In the Japanese story, the main character's adventures come through chance or fate. His or her rewards come from the kindness or goodness demonstrated throughout the story. Cultural bias in the story text may lead to testing bias.

The structure of English discourse is usually straightforward. The story starts at Point A and continues until Point Z is reached. There are very few digressions. Many cultures, however, have discourse styles that reflect their cultures and are highly different. Just as certain cultural amenities (sipping tea as a prelude to business) must be conducted in oral speech, so must they be conducted in writing in certain cultures. To go straight from Point A to Point Z would show rudeness (in Oriental cultures which tend to move in non-linear fashion) and a total lack of writing ability in Spanish (where the author likes to demonstrate his linguistic abilities through complex use of language).

SKILL 11.4 Demonstrate knowledge of assessment issues related to ELL students who may have a disability or who may be gifted and talented

Some of the characteristics of learning a second language seem to be the same characteristics shown by those with learning disabilities. This overlap has resulted in an over-representation of ELLs in the exceptional groupings (Ortiz & Garcia, 1995). While learning another language, students may show apparent processing difficulties, behavioral differences, reading difficulties, and expressive difficulties (Lock & Layton, 2002). Only careful observation can determine if they are natural language learning difficulties or, in fact, learning disabilities.

Before students can be classified as students with disabilities (SWDs) and referred to special education classes, their previous learning experiences should be analyzed using ESOL techniques. Also, any interventions should be documented and implemented for up to 10 weeks (Burnette, 1998; Rodriguez & Carrasquillo, 1997). The analysis of the results of early intervention strategies should make allowances for typical second language difficulties (Almandos & Petzold, 2001).

Teachers should be able to recognize the following characteristics as possible signs of giftedness in LEP students so that when one or more of these are present to a significant degree, the student is referred for screening and possible evaluation. The following characteristics are often seen among students who are ELLs, yet intellectually advanced:

- successful history in previous school setting
- advanced developmental history based on information provided in parent/guardian interview
- rapidity of learning
- ability to solve problems that are not dependent on English (e.g. putting complex pieces together to make a whole, sorting according to complex attributes, or doing mathematical calculations)
- high academic performance in tasks using heritage language
- successful history in environments where heritage language is required

SKILL 11.5 Demonstrate knowledge of different types of assessment (e.g., norm-referenced, criterion-referenced), including differences between performance-based and traditional assessments

Norm-referenced tests are those tests in which the results are interpreted based upon the performance of a given group, the norm. The norm group is a large group of individuals who are similar to the group being tested. Norm-referenced test results may be compared with the norm group using the mean and standard deviations or may be reported based solely upon the actual group being tested. The latter is referred to as grading on the curve.

Criterion-referenced tests are those where the individual's test score is based upon the mastery of course content. In this type of testing, it is possible for all participants to receive the highest score regardless of how many students achieve this grade.

Another category of testing refers to the first, second and third generation language tests. The first generation tests approximate the grammar-translation approach to teaching language, where the student is asked to perform tasks (e.g. write an essay, answer multiple choice questions). Such questions are typically devoid of context and are not authentic. Second generation tests (**traditional tests**) are based on discrete points, are typically very long, and many of the items may have no connection with each other.

They are often criticized precisely because of a lack of integrative language. Third generation tests (**performance-based tests**) are based upon the communicative principles and by their very nature are authentic. Examples would be listening to an airport announcement to find the time of arrival of a particular flight or writing notes from an authentic reading. The nature of the tasks requires the students to use language in an integrative form.

The strengths and weaknesses of the second and third generation tests make them suitable for different testing purposes.

SKILL 11.6   Demonstrate knowledge of various purposes of assessment (e.g., diagnosis, placement, evaluation of content-area achievement, evaluation of language proficiency, evaluation of instruction, program evaluation), including the difference between formative and summative assessment, and apply knowledge of strategies for selecting assessment(s) appropriate for an identified purpose

There are a multitude of tests for evaluating, assessing, and placing of ELLs in appropriate programs. Each test can test a narrow range of language skills (such as discrete tests designed to measure grammar sub-skills or vocabulary).

Language tests should be chosen on the basis of the information they give, the appropriateness of each instrument for the purpose, and the soundness of the test content. Language has over two hundred dimensions which can be evaluated, and yet most tests assess less than twelve of them. Therefore, all language testing should be done cautiously, backed up by teacher observations, oral interviews, family life variables, and school records.

Language placement tests:
A language placement test is designed to place a student within a specific program. The school district may design its own instrument or use a standardized test.

Language proficiency tests:
These tests measure how well students have met certain standards in a particular language. The standards have been predetermined and are unrelated to any course of study, curriculum or program. These tests are frequently used to enter or exit a particular program.

Examples are:

- ACTFL Oral Proficiency Interview (OPI)
- Test of Spoken English (TSE)
- Test of English as a Foreign Language (TOEFL)
- Foreign Service Exam (FSI)
- Oral Language Proficiency Scale from Miami-Dade County Public Schools

Language achievement tests:

These tests are related directly to a specific curriculum or course of study. The test includes language sub-skills, reading comprehension, parts of speech, and other mechanical parts of the language such as spelling, punctuation and paragraphing.

Examples are:

- unit exams
- final exams

Diagnostic language tests:

These tests are designed to identify individual students' strengths and weaknesses in languages. They are generally administered by speech therapists or psychologists in clinical settings when specific language learning problems are present.

SKILL 11.7 Demonstrate knowledge of national and state requirements for identifying, reclassifying, and exiting ELL students from language support programs and recognize how to apply this knowledge to make informed decisions regarding placement and reclassification of students in ESOL programs

ELLs are those whose primary or home language is other than English (PHLOTE) and are therefore, qualified for special services or language assistance language programs. All Georgia English Language Learners (ELLs) are tested annually in order to determine their proficiency level. These tests also provide the test administrators with information needed to meet federal and state requirements in student assessment.

All ELLs are required to participate in assessment programs, though a one-year deferment to students enrolled in U.S. school for the first time may be granted. This allows the ELL to be exempt from content area assessment, other than mathematics or science, if the ELL's proficiency suggests that testing is not in the best educational interests of the student.

The criteria for ending special services for English language learners and placing them in mainstream English-only classes as fluent English speakers is usually based on a combination of performance on an English language proficiency test and grades, standardized test scores, or teacher recommendations. In some cases, this re-designation of students may be based on the amount of time they have been in special programs.

To determine the eligibility of ELLs, the state of Georgia uses the World-Class Instructional Design and Assessment (WIDA) Consortium (See the WIDA website at www.wida.us). Each WIDA test assesses students' abilities in all four language domains (Listening, Speaking, Writing, and Reading), and evaluates social and instructional English as well as academic language corresponding to the subject areas of language arts, mathematics, science, and social studies. This screening tool is used to determine whether or not a child is eligible for English language instructional services. These assessments will be used to determine eligibility for language assistance when utilized in conjunction with the narrative GaDOE Eligibility Guidance below and/or the GaDOE Title III /ESOL Eligibility Flow Charts also available in this document.

(Adapted from: **Georgia Department of Education, Title III ESOL Resource Guide 2009-2010.**)

SKILL 11.8 Demonstrate knowledge of assessment and ways to apply this knowledge to select or design valid, reliable performance-based and traditional assessments for different purposes in the ESOL classroom

Certain factors may affect the assessment of ELLs who are not familiar with assessment in the U.S. or Georgia classroom. Among these is unfamiliarity with standard testing techniques. Students may become disconcerted when they are not allowed to ask questions of the teacher, are restricted by time constraints, or are not permitted to work on certain sections of the test at a time.

Students may also be uncomfortable when ELLs are allowed specific accommodation during the test session. Accommodations allowed by the test publisher or those prescribed by the state of Florida need to be introduced in the regular classroom, so that ELLs and other students are familiar with them before the testing session begins.

The constructs of reliability and validity are crucial in assessing ELLs because of the high stakes involved in testing in today's schools. Decisions about schools, teachers, and students are based on these tests. A reliable assessment test for ELLs will have the following three attributes: validity, reliability and practicality.

Validity: An assessment test can only be considered "valid", if it measures what it asserts to measure. If an ELL assessment test claims to measure oral proficiency, then the test should include a section where instructors ask the ELL to pronounce certain words, listen to the instructor's pronunciation and determine if it is correct, and/or respond directly to the instructor's questions.

According to Diaz-Rico and Weed (1995), *"...empirical validity is a measure of how effectively a test relates to some other known measure."* There are different types of validity: predictive and concurrent (Diaz-Rico & Weed, 1995.). "Predictive" empirical validity is concerned with the possible outcomes of test performance, while, "concurrent" empirical validity is connected with another variable for measurement. For example, if a learner shows a high amount of English speech proficiency in class, then the instructor would have the expectation that the learner would perform well during an oral proficiency exam.

Avalos (in Schumm: *Reading Assessment and Instruction for All Learners*, 2006.) states there are four types of bias which can affect validity:

- **Cultural bias:** Concerns acquired knowledge from participating in and sharing certain cultural values and experiences. Asking questions about birthdays or holiday celebrations presumes a middle-class family experience. Immigrants frequently do not celebrate birthdays because they live in poverty or perhaps because they celebrate the birthday differently (e.g., with an extended family and piñatas).
- **Attitudinal bias:** This refers to the negative attitude of the examiner towards a certain language, dialect, or culture. Just as low expectations from instructors can cause low results (the Pygmalion effect), the same thing happens during testing when a negative attitude conveyed by the assessor, teacher, or school culture can have negative results on the test results.
- **Test bias or norming bias:** This type of bias refers to excluding ELLs or different populations from the school's population used to obtain the norm results.
- **Translation bias:** Occurs when the test is literally translated from L2 to L1 by interpreters or other means. The "essence" of the test may be lost in such translation because it is difficult to translate cultural concepts.

Reliability: An assessment test can only be considered "reliable", if similar scores result when the test is taken a second time. Factors such as anxiety, hunger, tiredness, and uncomfortable environmental conditions should not cause a huge fluctuation in the learner's score. Typically, if a learner earns a score of 90% on a test which was created by the instructor, then averages predict that the learner probably scored 45% on one half of the test and 45% on the other half, regardless of the structure of the test items.

Practicality: A test which proves to be both valid and reliable may unfortunately prove to be cost or time-prohibitive. The ideal assessment test would be one that is easy to administer and easy to grade, as well as one that includes testing items closely similar to what the learners have experienced in class. However, when learners encounter test items such as writing journals, practicality becomes an issue. A writing journal, although an excellent method for learners to explore their critical literacy skills as well as track language achievement progress, can be difficult to grade due to the subjective content, nor may it be a fair representation of what the learners have encountered in class.

COMPETENCY 12.0   **Understand how to select and use multiple assessment strategies, techniques, and instruments, including analyzing and interpreting assessment results to inform, evaluate, and modify instruction for ELL students.**

SKILL 12.1   **Recognize how to select and use a variety of assessments that correspond with state and national standards for ESOL and specific content areas**

All ELLs are required to participate in all content area testing except those enrolled in a U.S. school system for less than one year. These ELLs may receive a one-time deferment in content area assessment, except for math and science.

ELLs may be given special accommodations, if warranted, for a maximum of two years after exiting ESOL or an alternative language assistance program.

The following three tests are among those used to test ELLs in Georgia:

- **Assessing Comprehension and Communication in English State to State for English Language Learners (ACCESS for ELLs)** – an English language proficiency test administered annually to all English language learners (ELLs) in Georgia for the purposes of determining the English language proficiency level of students; providing districts with information that will help them evaluate the effectiveness of their ESOL programs; providing information that enhances instruction and learning in programs for English language learners; assessing the annual English language proficiency gains using a standards-based assessment instrument; and providing data for meeting federal and state requirements with respect to student assessment

- **Georgia Alternate Assessment (GAA) – a portfolio assessment designed for students with significant cognitive disab**ilities under the Individuals with Disabilities Education Act (IDEA), i.e., students whose IEP team has determined they are unable to reasonably participate in the regular assessment program. The purpose of the GAA is to ensure all students, including students with significant cognitive disabilities, are provided access to the state curriculum and given the opportunity to demonstrate progress toward achievement of the state standards.

- **Language Proficiency Assessment** – an assessment of an ELL student's: (1) progress in the acquisition of the English language in the areas of listening, speaking, reading and writing; and (2) attainment of a prescribed level of performance in listening, speaking, reading, and writing to enable the student to communicate independently in both social and academic settings

SKILL 12.2 Recognize how to select assessments, including technology-based, self-, and peer-assessments, that are appropriate for ELL students at varying levels of English language proficiency and literacy development

The different types of assessments available to instructors in ESOL include:

- **Technology-based:** Technology-based assessments should be chosen with the content area needs in mind since technology should be used to support the curriculum and not as an end in itself. The ESOL instructor must determine if the assessment is based on directed models of learning (behaviorist, information-processing, cognitive-behavioral or systems theories) or on constructivist models (social activism, child development, or multiple intelligences theories). Keeping these theories in mind, the ESOL instructor can select software that will suit the needs of her ELLs.

- **Self assessment:** May be used to build autonomous and self-directed language learners, and to alleviate the assessment burden on teachers. Information gathered in these assessments may provide useful information on ELL's expectations and needs, their problems and worries, how they feel about their own progress, as well as their reactions to the materials and the course in general. (Harris and McCann, 1994: 63).

  Some problems associated with self assessment are: Difficulty in application where grades are of primary concern and there is completion. Another problem is the amount of time associated with training students in self-assessment techniques. A third problem is reliability.

- **Peer assessment:** Peer assessment may be achieved by having two students work together to review each other's work based on previously agreed-upon band scales or specific points the ESOL instructor is working on. As each ELL reviews his partner's work, he makes notes on 3" x 5" index cards and attaches them to the paper.

SKILL 12.3 Recognize how to select and use a variety of oral language assessments; analyze and interpret results from these assessments; use this information to inform, evaluate, and modify instruction related to ELL students' oral-language development

Weir (1993:30) suggests a three-part framework for constructing an oral evaluation of ELLs, which includes:

- the operations: activities (e.g. information routines such as telling a story) and skills (e.g. asking for clarification, if necessary) that are involved in the assessment
- the conditions under which the task is performed (e.g. time constraints, number of people involved and their familiarity with each other)
- the quality of output: the expected level of performance in terms of relevant criteria (e.g. accuracy, fluency, or intelligibility)

Based on the information received, ESOL instructors can develop information relevant to the needs of their ELLs.

SKILL 12.4 Recognize how to select and use a variety of reading assessments; analyze and interpret results from these assessments; use this information to inform, evaluate, and modify instruction related to ELL students' reading development

The use of authentic texts – text types associated with real purpose – has become increasingly popular in testing reading and listening skills for ELLs. Selecting the task type which will be important to an ELL as their language develops is also important. Some of the test formats that are useful for reading are:

- gap filling
- information transfer tasks (e.g. transferring information to tables or short answers)
- Cloze summaries
- summarizing main points of a text in a list
- writing answers to questions based on a text
- completing a text with information from a chart
  (Adapted from Weir, 1993)

SKILL 12.5 Recognize how to select and use a variety of writing assessments; analyze and interpret results from these assessments; use this information to inform, evaluate, and modify instruction related to ELL students' writing development

A major problem in assessing writing is to distinguish between the product approach and the process approach to writing and its assessment. Once a decision is made about the approach being used in the classroom, the ESOL instructor can determine which of the following activities is appropriate for the ELLs:

- gap filling
- form completion
- editing text
- open-ended essay
- responding to information given (e.g. in a letter, in chart form or other resources)
- information transfer tasks (e.g. transferring information to tables or short answers)
- summarizing specified points in a text
  (Adapted from Weir, 1993)

SKILL 12.6 Recognize how to select and use a variety of content-area assessments; analyze and interpret results from these assessments; use this information to inform, evaluate, and modify instruction related to ELL students' content-area knowledge

Content-area assessments are a challenge to ELLs because they usually require the student to read and then respond, or to express their understanding of concepts and procedures through writing. Since academic language in the content areas usually takes five to seven years to master, (compared with communicative language, which is much more quickly mastered), O'Malley and Pierce recommend scaffolding techniques to reduce the language demands on ELLs by:

- **exhibits or projects:** ELLs can be involved in presenting projects or demonstrations that illustrate the concepts or procedures being tested.
- **visual displays:** ELLs can use graphic organizers (e.g. diagrams or semantic maps) to illustrate their understanding of vocabulary and concepts.
- **organized lists:** ELLs can present lists of concepts or terms and demonstrate understanding by organizing or sequencing them.
- **tables or graphs:** ELLs can complete or construct and label tables and graphs to demonstrate their understanding of how data is organized and interpreted
- **short answers:** ELLs can give short answers or explanations that focus on the content area concepts.
  (Adapted from O'Malley and Pierce, 1996).

SUBAREA 4.0   **ESOL INSTRUCTION**

COMPETENCY 13.0   **Understand current trends, issues, and research-based practices related to promoting ELL students' oral language development.**

SKILL 13.1   **Demonstrate knowledge of activities and strategies that build and expand on ELL students' oral language experiences, situations, and interactions both inside and outside the classroom (e.g., following simple commands, formulating and answering yes/no and wh-questions, interviewing, inferring meaning of utterances, understanding idioms and figurative language)**

Communicative language competence has been the dominate paradigm for more than two decades. Even so, it is not without its critics who feel that the other three language skills (listening, reading, and writing) as well as content areas of the curriculum, have suffered as a consequence. For the foreseeable future, however, speaking will probably continue to be the most important skill for teachers and students alike.

McDonough and Shaw (1993: 152) enumerate our reason for speaking as follows:

- to express ideas and opinions
- to express a wish or desire
- to negotiate and/or solve a problem
- to establish and maintain social relationships

The teacher is a fundamental source of modeling language for ELLs when the language is authentic. Yet all too often, the language between the teacher and the student gives little room for authentic communication, relying instead on the traditional three-part exchange: teacher's initial move, learner's response, and the teacher's follow-up move (Sinclair and Coulthard, 1975).

Some of the activities that teachers can do to encourage more oral production from the ELLs in authentic situations are:

- **Total Physical Response (TPR):** The teacher or a chosen student gives commands to which students must respond to show understanding. The children's game "Simon Says" may be used with students of all ages by increasing the stakes (e.g. Give the commands at faster rate or make them more complex, always keeping in mind the ability level of the ELLs).
- **Group work:** encourages authentic language when ELLs ask for clarification, participate in discussions, interrupt each other, compete for the floor, and kid around. Group work also encourages learner autonomy.

- **Task-based activities:** require the members of the group to achieve an objective and express it in notes, rearrangement of jumbled items, a drawing, or a spoken summary.
  Ellis (1994: 596-598) concluded that two-way exchanges of information show more benefits:

  - Two-way tasks require more negotiation of meaning.
  - ELLs usually produce more complex and more target-like language when they have sufficient time to plan their responses.
  - Closed tasks (those with one single, correct solution) produce more negotiation work than those which have no predetermined solution.

SKILL 13.2 Recognize how to use a variety of meaningful, purposeful activities for developing ELL students' communicative competence (e.g., paired and small-group conversations and discussions, creative drama, role-play, oral presentations)

Discussion activities:

- **Describing pictures:** Each group has a picture that all members of the group can see. The secretary makes a check for each sentence the members of the group can say describing the picture. (The secretary does not have to write out the sentence.) After two minutes, the checks are added up, and the group tries to surpass their checks by describing a second picture.
- **Picture differences:** Each pair is given a set of two pictures. Without showing their pictures to their partners, they must find out what differences there are in the pictures.
- **Solving a problem:** Students are told that they will be on an educational advisory committee, which has to advise the principal on a problem with students. They should discuss their recommendations and write them out as a letter to the principal. (The teacher needs to prepare the problem and copy it for each student or group.)

Creative drama: This activity can be used in the language classroom to encourage dialogue technique. Students either write their own play or learn one from English literature. The activity is time consuming, but increases the confidence and morale of ELLs.

Role plays and skits: ELLs are each given a card with a situation in addition to a task or problem. The participants can be given time to practice their role play or they may improvise. This activity is usually done in pairs or small groups.
(Adapted from Ur, 1996.)

SKILL 13.3 Demonstrate knowledge of strategies for developing ELL students' listening skills for a variety of academic and social purposes (e.g., responding appropriately to multiple-step directions or taking notes on an unfamiliar topic)

Ur (1996) lists some of the occasions on which we listen and appropriately respond:

- interview questions
- instructions
- loudspeaker announcements
- radio news
- committee meetings
- shopping
- at the theater
- on the telephone
- lessons or lectures
- conversation and gossip
- television
- storytelling

Most of these situations use language that is informal and spontaneous. In the classroom, teachers are training ELLs for real-life listening situations. Bearing this in mind, the most useful types of activities are those where the listener (ELL) is asked to listen to genuinely informal talk instead of the typical written text. The speaker should be visible to the listener and there should be direct speaker-listener interaction. Finally, there should only be one exposure to the text as in real-life the listener will rarely have the opportunity to have the text "replayed.'"

The tasks themselves should be presented in such a way that the ELL can use his or her previous knowledge to anticipate outcomes. Saying, "You are going to hear a husband and wife discuss summer vacation plans" is far more useful than merely stating, "Listen to the passage…". Also, the ELLs should be given a task to complete as they listen (e.g. Listen for where they are planning to go. Mark this on your map.) Finally, the ELLs should be permitted to answer the questions as they hear the information and not wait until the end.
(Adapted from Ur, 1996.)

SKILL 13.4 **Demonstrate knowledge of strategies for developing ELL students' speaking skills for a variety of academic and social purposes and audiences (e.g., using appropriate intonation, stress, and pronunciation at the word, phrase, and extended discourse levels; engaging in conversations and academic discussions using language appropriate to the situation and topic)**

For most native-speaking teachers, modeling language for the ELL student is an extremely important part of language learning. However, there are specific issues that the ELLs need to address in order to improve their language skills. Pronunciation includes the sounds of the language, or its phonology and intonation, in addition to its stress and rhythm patterns.

Pronunciation: To work on pronunciation, ELLs can take a dictionary and study its phonetic alphabet. Once they are familiar with it, they can take 10-12 words from a book and try to transcribe them and then pronounce them.

Intonation: Some researchers doubt if this can be taught (Barnes, 1988). However, it is important because the message may be misconstrued if the speaker uses an incorrect intonation pattern. One exercise is for ELLs to listen to a passage and mark the intonation pattern using forward slashes or backward slashes over the syllables or words to indicate a rising or falling pattern. Other people use curved lines to indicate the appropriate rising and falling of the voice.

Stress: Stress means accent. To teach ELLs the accent of words, dictionary assignments may be used. For sentences or longer texts, the ELLs can mark the stress on the words or syllables as the teacher dictates a short passage to them.

SKILL 13.5 **Recognize the role of oral language development in literacy and content-area instruction (e.g., formulating questions based on understanding of classroom lectures, comprehending concrete and abstract topics, recognizing language subtleties)**

Students must be given the opportunities to practice oral language in the academic classroom. To develop their oral language skills, ELLs need to have time for self-correction without pressure. In exercises where accuracy is the focus, ELLs need correction soon after the mistakes occur, but in other instances, when ELLs need to practice their fluency, the teacher may withhold correction. Teachers should concentrate only on selective mistakes for correction.

The role of the instructor is to model the academic language. The teacher should model the correct technical language (e.g. of science, math, literature et al.) and grammatical structure. Nevertheless, if necessary, the instructor should paraphrase, define, and give examples to help ELLs understand what is being instructed. The use of cooperative learning activities, group projects, and hands-on activities give ELLs the opportunity to practice oral language skills in content areas.

COMPETENCY 14.0   Understand foundations of literacy development in ESOL, including current trends, issues, policies, and research-based practices related to ESOL instruction in literacy development

SKILL 14.1   Recognize orthographic, linguistic, and rhetorical influences of L1 on ELL students' English literacy development (e.g., positive and negative transfer from L1)

Corder is most noted for his work in "error analysis," a field that until 1970 was not fully recognized (Ellis, 1994.) Corder drew a line, separating errors of skill (competency) from errors in presentation (performance). Richards (1971) cites the following reasons for learner errors:

- **L1 transfers:** L1 transfer or L1 interference occurs when a learner's primary language L1 influences his or her progress in L2. Pronunciation, grammar structures, vocabulary, and semantics are commonly affected.

- **Overgeneralization:** Overgeneralization occurs when the learner attempts to apply a grammatical rule to instances where it does not apply. For example, a learner is overgeneralizing when he or she applies a grammatical rule to all verbs and does not account for exceptions, e.g., the learner adds "ed" to the verb "go" to form the past tense, rather than using "went."

- **Simplification:** The practice of modifying language to facilitate comprehension may actually delay growth. Researchers disagree on the value of this practice. Krashen believes that simplification aids L2 acquisition. Others believe that lessening authentic texts diminishes L2 learners' ability to comprehend more difficult texts.

Correcting lexical errors ("No, that's not a house; it's a skyscraper") contributes to language learning. However, correcting every grammatical error creates a negative atmosphere that makes students afraid to express themselves for fear of making a mistake and being corrected. Students also lose fluency if they try to analyze rules and grammar before speaking.

The problem of identifying learners' misconceptions hinges on making a correct analysis and diagnosis of the learners' input. Teachers often misinterpret the intended meaning of a learner's speech. Teachers have believed that if they are familiar with students and their first language, they are more likely to guess a learner's intended meaning. This approach assumes that errors in English differ according to the learner's first language and that understanding common types of errors typical of a particular first language can help a teacher to approach student errors more effectively and provide focused practice. For example, Spanish speakers often pronounce the consonant "s" as "es" because many Spanish words begin this way. The word for "study" in Spanish is "estudiar" And "student" is "estudiante". A teacher can cluster these words and create ways to practice this type of word.

However, an alternative, cognitive approach uses general knowledge which can be applicable to a variety of languages. This approach uses a unifying linguistic theory which encompasses all human languages in a universal framework. It describes languages as a set of interlocking principles and introduces parameters to account for the variations amongst languages. In this approach, the diagnoses are made following some patterns of acquisition that this theory defines, mirroring the language acquisition process.

Research has shown the traditional practice of correcting written work by providing a corrected version to be ineffective. Students cannot integrate large numbers of corrections into their cognitive processes, and visually, a page with as much teacher as student writing demoralizes a student who has made a concerted effort to express ideas. A better approach is to note one example each of up to three types of errors and explain to the individual or the class if many learners make the same type of error, proper usage.

SKILL 14.2   Demonstrate knowledge of specific literacy needs of ELL students (e.g., students with limited literacy in L1) and strategies for addressing those needs

Research suggests that, contrary to many popular myths, immigrant children, poor families, and other minority group families do value literacy and education. Although literacy varies in different families, literacy serves many functions in families living below the poverty level, families in which English is not the primary language, and families with low educational levels (Peregoy and Boyle, 2008). Teachers need to be perceptive and draw upon the child's home language and literacy experiences so that the child is better served when beginning literacy instruction.

Encouraging home involvement in the literacy process is critical. Family members model reading and writing every time they read the newspaper or magazine, make a shopping list, note an appointment on a calendar, review their work schedule, or discuss the newest charges on the phone bill. Many children come from societies where oral storytelling traditions (e.g. Navajo, Spanish, Hmong, or African-American) provide excellent foundations for literacy development.

Nevertheless, little research has been conducted about how to teach ELLs with limited literacy in their first language while learning a second language—whether a young child or an older one. If feasible, students should first learn to read in their native language and later the second language. When instruction is begun in English, many ESOL practitioners believe that the same methods used to teach the native speaker will be beneficial to the ELL because similar literacy patterns will probably emerge. Older learners may be able to progress more rapidly because they use their worldly experiences to help them with comprehension and communication.

National reading authorities recommend phonemic awareness, phonics, reading fluency, and comprehension as the keys to success in achieving literacy. All of these elements should be considered within meaningful contexts rather than in isolation. Instruction in specific strategies (e. g. summarizing, retelling, answering questions) will help ELLs become independent readers and writers.

SKILL 14.3 Recognize the components of a balanced, comprehensive reading program for ELL Students

For beginning readers who are ELLs, the importance of a balanced but comprehensive reading program cannot be emphasized enough. The National Council of Teachers of English states that there is a close relationship between oral language and reading. Current theories of literacy development suggest that we develop literacy in the same way we develop oral language, i.e., through comprehensible input.

Huck, Heppler, & Hickman (1987) claim that, "Literature asks universal questions about the meaning of life and human relationships with nature and other people." Thus, literature can enrich the students' lives and augment their general knowledge of other cultures as they learn about the characters in stories and the world in which they live. While they are listening to or reading a story, students derive esthetic pleasure from the story. When asked to repeat the story, they are able to use similar language and language patterns as the stories they are retelling (Hade, 1988).

Slavin and Cheung (2003) state that the best reading programs for ELLs are probably similar to those of first language learners with appropriate adaptations to their language proficiency. These programs (for both elementary and secondary school students) include such elements as:

- systematic phonics instruction
- quality instruction
- cooperative learning
- cognitive strategy instruction
- one-to-one tutoring for ELLs who are struggling in reading
- direct teaching of English vocabulary
- reading a wide range of grade-appropriate books

SKILL 14.4   Recognize the importance of applying knowledge of the developmental process of reading in a second language to design standards-based reading instruction adapted to and appropriate for ELL students (e.g., selecting and using different texts and genres for ELL students at different proficiency levels and developmental stages, using both literature and content-area texts to develop ELL students' reading skills)

Children learn to read only once. If they are able to read in their native language, they are able to read in English. It is important for ELLs to increase their vocabulary and knowledge of the structure of English, their second language. By building on what the ELL already knows with regard to literacy, language, and experiences in his or her native language, teachers will be able to improve the reading level of the ELL in English. For this reason, it is necessary to evaluate the ELL in his or her first, native, or heritage language in order to initiate the best reading instruction in English.

Reading stages were first studied by Chall (1983). She proposed six stages of reading that change over time as children progress through school.

- Pre-reading: typical of preschool through late kindergarten (also called pre-alphabetic, logographic, pre-conventional)
- Initial reading or alphabetic decoding: typical of kindergarten through early second grade (also called alphabetic decoding stage)
- Confirmation and fluency: typical of second and third grades
- Reading to learn: typical of fourth to eighth grades
- Multiple points of view: typical of high school
- Construction and reconstruction: typical of college and adulthood

Newer studies emphasize the integration of processing skills and the importance of sound, spelling, and meaning in learning words. These elements develop together on a continuum. Rich text environments are crucial to the growth process.

Ehri (1996) developed a continuum of word reading development demonstrating how children master the alphabetic principle. Children cannot retain more than a few dozen sight words and progress is developed only if they are able to relate letters to sounds. For many ELLs, this process is particularly difficult if their language is phonetic, since English is not. English has roughly forty-four sounds corresponding to twenty-six letters while Spanish, for example, has direct letter-sound correspondence. For phonetic readers, decoding English words can be difficult.

- The Logographic Phase: The child may
  - try to remember words by incidental visual characteristics
  - treat words as pictograms and make a direct association to meaning
  - equate the length of the word with its meaning

- The Novice Alphabetic Phase: The child may
  - identify the first consonant in a word; must learn to separate all sounds
  - rely on letter names to identify word; needs to distinguish between letter sounds and their names
  - confuse similar words; needs to decode the whole word, left to right, with sound-symbol link

- The Mature Alphabetic Phase: The child
  - can sound out regular one-syllable words
  - can increase speed of whole word recognition when decoding becomes accurate
  - has well established phonemic awareness
  - can represent almost every sound with a logical letter choice
  - can represent and recognize spelling patterns, words of more than one syllable, meaningful parts of words and basic sight vocabulary

- The Orthographic Phase: The child can
  - read words using phonemes, syllabic units, morpheme units, and whole words
  - use sequential and hierarchical decoding, i.e. notices familiar parts first then decodes unfamiliar parts
  - remember multisyllabic words
  - use knowledge of word origin, syntactic roles, ending rules, prefixes, suffixes, and root forms to decode words and their meanings

Students who are proficient readers in L1 have more reading success in L2 (Collier & Thomas, 1989: Ovando et al, 2003; and Snow, Burns & Griffin, 1998). This fact leads us to the question, "What role does the oral second language play in the reading process?" In general, bilingual education models maintain the idea that ELLs be at least at the level of speech emergence before reading instruction begins. However, given the increasing variation of the U.S. school population, many believe that it is no longer equitable to wait for oral proficiency before beginning reading instruction. Anderson & Roit (1998) argue that reading instruction should be used with certain L2 learners and avoided with others. When instruction is well planned and teachers consider the individual students' needs, all ELLs can benefit from reading instruction in L2.

SKILL 14.5 **Recognize the importance of applying knowledge of the developmental process of writing in a second language to design standards-based writing instruction adapted to and appropriate for ELL students (e.g., developing ELL students' writing through a range of activities from basic sentence construction to narrative, expository, and persuasive writing, including responses to literature using different genres for ELL students at different proficiency levels and developmental stages; using different genres to meet different social needs and academic demands; providing explicit instruction regarding contrasts between English and the writing systems of ELL students' home language)**

Just as the native English speaker has to manage many different skills to become a proficient writer, so must the ELL student. These skills include clarity of thought and expression and how to use different genres to convey different purposes in writing as well as conventional spelling, grammar, and punctuation. Since these skills vary, as do the traits of each specific type of writing, it is not easy to discuss writing stages. Even so, it is important for teachers to have a general guide on which to base their instruction plans.

The following chart, based on a writing matrix developed by Peregoy and Boyle (2008), offers a good guide to identifying characteristics of a student's writing level. It encompasses three developmental levels and six traits.

- Trait 1: Fluency
  Beginning Level: Writes one or two short sentences.
  Intermediate Level: Writes several sentences.
  Advanced Level: Writes a paragraph or more.

- Trait 2: Organization
  Beginning Level: Lacks logical sequence or is so short that organization presents no problem.
  Intermediate Level: Writing is somewhat sequenced.
  Advanced Level: Writing follows standard organization for genre.

- Trait 3: Grammar
  Beginning Level: Student demonstrates basic word-order problems, uses only present tense form.
  Intermediate Level: Student makes minor grammatical errors.
  Advanced Level: Grammar resembles that of native speaker of same age.

- Trait 4: Vocabulary
Beginning Level: Student has limited vocabulary, needs to rely at times on L1 or ask for translation.
Intermediate Level: Student knows most words needed to express ideas but lacks vocabulary for finer shades of meaning.
Advanced Level: Student is flexible in word choice; similar to good native writer of the same age.

- Trait 5: Genre
Beginning Level: Student does not differentiate form to suit purpose.
Intermediate Level: Student chooses form to suit purpose but is limited in choices of expository forms.
Advanced Level: Student knows several genres, makes appropriate choices similar to effective native writers of same age.

- Trait 6: Sentence variety
Beginning Level: Student uses one or two sentence patterns.
Intermediate Level: Student uses several sentence patterns.
Advanced Level: Student uses a good variety of sentence patterns effectively.

COMPETENCY 15.0   **Understand approaches, methods, and strategies for promoting ELL students' literacy development**

SKILL 15.1   **Demonstrate knowledge of the importance of building on the languages the students bring to the classroom to promote their literacy development**

Peregoy & Boyle (2008) state that literacy scaffolding helps ELLs with reading and writing at a level that would be impossible for them otherwise. Scaffolding allows ELLs to work at their level in both reading and writing, and at the same time, challenges them to reach their next level of development. To help students achieve their level, several criteria are suggested:

- use of functional, meaningful communication found in whole texts
- use of language and discourse patterns that repeat themselves and are predictable
- a model (from teacher or peers) for understanding and producing particular written language patterns
- support for students at a level Krashen refers to as $i + 1$.
- supports discarded when the student no longer needs them.

Keeping in mind the scaffolding theory, teachers may use the first language in instruction—when they know it. This is not always possible. In many states, there are hundreds of language communities represented in the statewide school system. A danger of first language use for instruction is that some students become dependent and are reluctant to utilize their knowledge of the second language. However, for most children, instruction in their first language has numerous advantages. First language instruction lowers the affective filter by reducing tension, anxiety, and even fear, thus permitting faster learning; it can clarify misunderstandings in the second language content, and it can be used to explain how the two languages differ or are the same with respect to different types of reading texts or writing tasks.

Teachers can also use the similarities and differences of the different languages to teach learning strategies. For example, the adjective normally comes before the noun in English but in Spanish it more frequently comes after the noun. A text written in English is expected to have a main idea and several supporting details to explain or support it. Other languages are more descriptive and depend on the beauty of the language to convey the writer's meaning. By using the concept of cognates, both true and false, teachers can improve vocabulary development.

SKILL 15.2 **Demonstrate knowledge of various approaches, methods, and strategies for promoting ELL students' English-language reading development and engagement in reading (e.g., Language Experience Approach, pre-teaching vocabulary and language structures, schema development, shared reading, guided reading, graphic organizers, literature circles, exposure to a variety of literature, maintaining personal spelling and vocabulary dictionaries)**

The **Language Experience Approach (LEA)** is an instructional technique used to encourage spoken responses from ELL students after they are exposed to a variety of first-hand, sensory experiences (Badia, 1966). LEA develops and improves the student's reading and writing skills by using their ideas and language. The following are eight steps for incorporating LEA into ELL curriculum (Dixon & Nessel, 1983):

Step 1: An "Experience" Story (Motivation):
An experience story is a story characterized as an "experience which is shared by both the student and teacher." The goal here is for the student's thinking and language production to be stimulated when retelling a story or experience.

Step 2: Facilitating the Language Process:
Once a student has finished telling a story or experience, the instructor should immediately initiate conversation.

Step 3: Creating a Personal View Representation
The individual draws or paints a picture to represent something interesting about the experience. The activity works best when there are six to eight students.

Step 4: Retelling Events/Reactions
A volunteer is selected to share his/her picture with the entire group. The teacher elicits from other students the parts they found interesting. Using the same vocabulary and syntax when possible, sentences are written on the board and later copied on chart paper or even in the students' notebooks (at higher levels).

Step 5: Writing Students' Statements
For this step, the teacher questions the students individually and writes their exact words on the board. After writing each statement on the board, the teacher reads it back to the class for confirmation of accuracy. The teacher should stop after every four or five statements to allow the students to organize the statements in sequential order. The statements are numbered and copied onto sentence strip paper. Students are then given the sentence strips to place in the chart holder.

Step 6: Reading
When the chart has been completed, each student reads his or her statement to the group and the teacher. Next the teacher reads the story, underlining each statement as it is read, moving from left to right. The entire group reads the story chorus fashion or volunteers may read it.

Step 7: Writing

Once the students have acquired writing skills, they can copy the stories onto lined paper or into their notebooks. Stories can be collected into a bound folder called "Our Stories."

Step 8: Follow-Up Activities

During the following days, the story may be read again by either the teacher or the students or both. ELLs can be asked to match letter, word, or sentence cards to the original story. Students may wish to illustrate or dramatize the story and present it to other classes, parents, or administrators.

Schemata need to be activated to draw upon the previous knowledge and learning of the ELL, especially when the ELL may not have had experiences similar to the mainstream culture. The use of graphics to encourage pre-reading thought about a topic (e.g., brainstorming, web maps, and organizational charts) activates this knowledge and shows how information is organized in the students' minds. Shumm (2006) states that research has shown:

- More prior knowledge permits a reader to understand and remember more (Brown, Bransford, Ferrara, & Campione, 1983).
- Prior knowledge must be activated to improve comprehension (Bransford & Johnson, 1972).
- Failure to activate prior knowledge is one cause of poor readers (Paris & Lindauer, 1976).
- Good readers accept new information if they are convinced by an author's arguments. Likewise, they may reject ideas when they conflict with a reader's prior knowledge (Pressley, 2000).

Teachers may organize students in pairs for **peer tutoring** (Schumm, 2006). The teacher becomes a facilitator who circulates, answering questions or clarifying pronunciation and meaning. The tutee (the more proficient reader) reads the text aloud. The tutor listens. The roles are reversed. The new tutor points out mistakes to the tutee and asks for corrections or asks if the tutee can figure it out. Students can retell the story to check for comprehension.

SKILL 15.3   Demonstrate knowledge of activities and strategies for promoting ELL students' achievement of state performance standards related to beginning reading development (e.g., developing phonological awareness skills, knowledge of the alphabetic principle, concepts about print, and phonemic awareness skills) and reading skills and strategies (e.g., decoding and word-recognition skills, including use of phonics, structural analysis, and context clues; application of grammar and punctuation to derive meaning; development of reading fluency; vocabulary development)

The International Reading Association (1997) issued a position statement on the place of phonics in reading instruction. This position paper asserts that phonics has an important place in beginning reading instruction, primary teachers value and teach phonics, and effective phonics is integrated into the total language arts program. To help children learn phonics, teaching analytical phonics in context seems to work better than teaching synthetic phonics in isolation, e.g., on worksheets.

Some of the techniques for beginning reading development, skills and strategies are glossed below.

- Teaching children to understand sentences, texts, and other materials is better than trying to teach word skills in isolation.
- Children can learn alphabetic principles by alphabetizing lists of spelling words or groups of objects.
- Simple techniques such as holding up the left hand and recognizing the letter 'L' can help children remember which side of the text to begin reading first.
- Learning to decode words is best achieved by practicing while reading.
- Sight words can be memorized.
- Three major types of context clues are: syntactic (word order, word endings, function of words in a sentence), semantic (meaning clues), and phonemes and graphemes (/ph/ may sound like /f/ as in photograph, /ch/ sometimes sounds like a /k/ as in chemistry).
- Reading fluency may be improved by observing the following strategies (et al.): reread for clarity and to improve understanding, ask for help when confused, realize that "There is no such thing as a stupid question." Venn diagrams, webs, and other graphics may be helpful in organizing texts for easier understanding.
- Vocabulary cards or dictionaries may help ELLs to recall words they don't know. Word walls and instruction on idioms, antonyms, synonyms, and homonyms are useful.
- Learning the structure of sentence patterns, question forms, and their punctuation can help the ELL to determine meaning.

SKILL 15.4 **Demonstrate knowledge of activities and strategies for promoting ELL students' achievement of state performance standards related to reading comprehension (e.g., identifying main topic and details in stories; using prior knowledge and context to construct meaning; reading and responding to different genres of literature; identifying plot, point of view, and theme; varying reading rate for different texts and different purposes for reading), including facilitating ELL students' reading comprehension before, during, and after reading; developing ELL students' literal, inferential, and critical/evaluative reading comprehension skills**

Many people wait for a reading passage to present information in an organized way for them. However, **reading comprehension** is a highly complex area where successful readers use reading strategies in each of the three distinct phases of reading—pre-reading, during reading, and post-reading—to successfully understand a text (Peregoy and Boyle, 2008).

- The purpose of the "pre-reading reading phase" is for teachers to build background knowledge through anticipation guides or field trips, motivate the reader with structured overviews or films, and establish the purpose of the reading using experiments or pictures.
- The purpose of the "during reading phase" is to read based upon the established purpose using learning logs or annotating texts to record information, improve comprehension by Directed Reading-Thinking Activities and asking questions, and utilize background knowledge by studying headings and subheadings and answering questions.
- The purpose of the "post-reading phase" is to help the student with organizing and remembering information through activities such as art work, maps, or summaries and to use the information in reporting, making a film, or publishing.

Some of the techniques students need to be able to master in reading comprehension include:

- skimming to extract main idea
- scanning for specific information
- predicting based upon prior knowledge
- restating the information to indicate comprehension of the text
- recognizing inferred information
- sounding out unfamiliar words and guessing at their meaning based upon previous understanding of the text
- summarizing the text

Teachers can guide students through these steps by using scaffolding techniques and giving guidance as needed.

Children's and juvenile literature includes parables, fables, fairy tales, folktales, myths, legends, novels, romances, poetry, drama, and novels. ELLs need to be taught the intricacies of plot, point of view, setting, characterization, and other literary terms just as their native speaking classmates do. Many of these terms are universals, but the instructor should be aware that the literature of other cultures may vary considerably from its English counterpart. Drawing on background knowledge of ELLs is valuable, but literary genre and terms will undoubtedly have to be taught. Encouraging and promoting wide reading of the different genre both inside and outside the classroom is one way to introduce these elements to the students.

SKILL 15.5 Demonstrate knowledge of various approaches, methods, and strategies for promoting ELL students' English-language writing development and engagement in writing (e.g., providing explicit instruction in the writing process, providing opportunities for ungraded writing such as interactive journals)

The writing process needs to be taught, since many students come from backgrounds where conventions for writing a text or paper are very different from the U.S. conventions. They are unfamiliar with the process of planning the paper, doing research, organizing the material, developing a thesis statement, deciding on methods of development, drafting, revising, and editing. Rubrics can be devised which are appropriate to process writing, taking into consideration both the process and the product.

There are many ways to get students to practice writing without grading the written product, such as learning logs, journals, and quick-writes. Teachers can devise prompts that allow ELLs to reflect on their learning and class discussions or explore new ideas. They may rewrite complex ideas in their own words and compare, evaluate, critique, or interpret. At the end of a period, students may quickly write what they learned during the class. ELLs can write dialog, either in pairs or individually. They can try using vocabulary words from their text in comprehensible paragraphs. Another idea is to write from the perspective of another person, place or thing (Adapted from: Zwiers, 2007).

SKILL 15.6 **Demonstrate knowledge of activities and strategies for promoting ELL students' achievement of state performance standards related to writing (e.g., sentence formation; paragraph formation; using compound and complex sentences; developing knowledge and skills in English writing conventions, mechanics, and spelling; applying appropriate rhetorical and discourse structures in writing across a range of genres)**

Students coming into the U.S. school system for the first time may have little idea of the writing process or how it is used. On the other hand, they may be fairly sophisticated in their manipulation of language. However, their language may value other aspects of writing that are very different from the U.S. idea of a sentence (s-v-o) or a paragraph (the topic sentence and its supporting details). In essays, the idea of developing sentences of varying lengths and structures, and connecting them through the skillful use of connectors will have to be taught through skillful modeling and use of examples. Supplying ample resources, such as dictionaries and lists of vocabulary conventions or connectors, will be invaluable to ELLs in upper levels.

Also, students who are learning to write need to read as much as possible of the genre that they are going to be writing about. As writing takes place in multiple genres (narrative prose, poetry, mathematical proofs, historical accounts, case studies, essays, emails, and letters), students should be exposed to each particular type of writing—its organization, the thinking behind the form, grammar, and the correct terms used in each genre—so that they are able to replicate the appropriate phrases and syntax in their writing. As non-mainstream students will not have had as much exposure to the models as native speakers, it is necessary to point out the conventions of each genre as it is studied in the classroom.

COMPETENCY 16.0   **Understand current trends, issues, and research-based practices related to promoting ELL students' content-area knowledge and skills.**

SKILL 16.1   Demonstrate knowledge of strategies for identifying and addressing specific academic needs of ELL students (e.g., limited formal schooling, gaps in prior knowledge, and need for concept development)

The ELLs who have arrived in the school system in upper elementary or secondary grades may have limited literacy skills or age-appropriate academic content knowledge in their native language. Academic language may be new and totally different from their previous experiences where they may have been forced to develop survival skills. Others may be from rural areas where they learned about life cycles, reproduction and weather. City dwellers may have been involved in the buying, selling, and bartering of goods. Even though the ELL may not know how to read or write, many cultures value literature handed down orally from generation to generation.

One way to bridge these gaps and difficulties is by using CALLA. The CALLA teacher needs to first introduce basic literacy skills. If possible, these should be introduced in the native or heritage language of the child. For older students, the Language Experience Approach has proven effective. Another technique to use with older students is to have them read such everyday items as signs, menus, ads, and recipes because there is an immediate association with these materials and the need to learn to read (Chamot & O'Malley, 1994).

SKILL 16.2   Demonstrate knowledge of strategies for activating ELL students' prior knowledge related to content-area objectives, including using knowledge of ELL students' home cultures to enhance learning

- **Illustrated autobiographies** ("All about Me" or "The Story of My Life") can help ease ELLs into the academic challenges of a new school and culture. Students use as much English as they can and draw pictures to illustrate other points. This is an integrative activity because ELLs are not singled out but part of the group.
- **Dialogue journals** can be used with students of all ages. Provide all students with blank journals and allow them to draw or write in the language of their choice. The instructor should respond to the journals periodically. Journals are an excellent way to develop a personal relationship with the students while introducing literacy to the class.
- **Themes** such as "Where We Were Born" or "Family Origins" make good starting points to bring in home cultures and activate the prior knowledge of all students (Adapted from Peregoy and Boyle, 2008).

SKILL 16.3 Demonstrate knowledge of strategies for contextualizing content and vocabulary (e.g., through demonstrations, illustrations) and for modifying language (e.g., repeating key concepts, breaking up long sentences, paraphrasing) to make content-area lessons accessible to ELL students

When providing contextualization, the instructor should:

- use facial expressions and gestures.
- use realia (cultural objects).
- use visual cues, such as pictures, blackboard sketches, DVDs, videos, slides, transparencies, etc.
- use graphic organizers.

When speaking, instructors should:

- speak slowly but naturally, taking care to enunciate without raising the volume.
- use short sentences when explaining a concept or instructions.
- use instructional strategies like repeating or rephrasing.
- write new vocabulary, expressions, or idioms on the board for further reinforcement.

When giving directions, the instructor should:

- simplify complicated tasks by giving specific instructions such as, "Open to page 107. Read the story. Once you have finished, wait for the class to finish reading."
- periodically check for comprehension during the lesson.
- provide opportunities for learner interactions.
- create cooperative learning groups. Cooperative learning groups are essential for LEP learners with varying levels of proficiency; "heterogeneous" groupings help to improve academic performance, especially if LEP students have the opportunity to clarify concepts and ask questions in their primary language.

SKILL 16.4 Identify strategies for integrating language and content objectives in ESOL instruction

In general, the ESOL teacher should focus on content and derive language activities from the content rather than letting the language and grammar determine the syllabus. In this way, the ELL is practicing the same academic language used in their grade-level content areas. Listening and reading strategies are very helpful for ELLs .(Chamot & O'Malley 1994).

Another key point is to select high-priority content to be covered in order to bring ELLs up to grade level. ELLs must understand the major concepts and skills taught in previous grades so that they are prepared for grade-level content. This process includes learning the major concepts, the skills, and the academic language associated with these areas. The ESOL instructor should aim for depth and not breadth of content.

SKILL16 .5   Demonstrate knowledge of content-based ESOL instructional methods that are effective in developing ELL students' academic language skills, content knowledge, and active participation in content areas

Theory: When learners are instructed through content-based instruction in areas such as mathematics, science, social studies, they tend to achieve a much higher proficiency level in the target language, than if they were only instructed in the TL through ESOL methods.

Strategy: The **Cognitive Academic Language Learning Approach (CALLA)** integrates the following tenets:

- The L2 learners' actual grade level in the main subject areas of mathematics, science, and social studies etc. should be the deciding factor for content.
- The L2 learners should be exposed to and gradually acquire the specific language used when studying in the subject areas, like: add this column of numbers, determine "x" in this algebraic problem, identify the properties of this cell, etc.
- The L2 learners' should be encouraged to use higher level cognitive processes, such as application, analysis and synthesis.

SKILL 16.6   Demonstrate knowledge of cognitive-learning strategies (e.g., organizational skills, study skills, test-taking skills) that support ELL students' development of content-related language, learning skills, and construction of academic knowledge

Organizational skills:

- Classifying: Students classify different objects according to size, shape, texture, etc.
- Comparing: Students can compare two objects, texts, or pictures using a Venn diagram or descriptive sentences or phrases.
- Ordering: Students arrange objects according to size, weight, height, or alphabetical order, etc. Events may be listed in chronological order, etc.
- Interpreting: Students can use and interpret charts, tables, graphs, maps, etc. in the acquisition of knowledge.

Study skills:

- **Note-taking skills:** For older students, have them divide their notebook page into a two-thirds and one-third page. The two-thirds portion is for notes on their reading and the one-third is for class notes on the same topic.

- **Time-management:**
  - Turn large tasks into smaller ones.
  - Keep a weekly schedule.
  - Use a student planner (or cell phone) to keep track of when assignments are due.
  - Make lists.
  - Stay flexible.

- **Read-study techniques:**
  - **KWL:** Set up a chart with a List of what you **Know**, what you **Want** to know, and what you **Learned**

Test-taking skills:

- A potential "workaround" to reduce the ELL's anxiety would be to administer practice tests, especially of multiple-choice or Cloze procedures with which they may not be familiar, to allow the ELL to develop a comfort level.
- ELLs may also need to learn U.S. testing techniques such as timed tests where time limits are not negotiable.
- ELLs may need to ask questions, or have certain test or text items read to them in order for them to understand the questions. (N.B. This is not appropriate for all testing situations, so practicing before such testing as "high-stakes'" testing is necessary.)

SKILL 16.7 Demonstrate knowledge of strategies for promoting ELL students' use of reference materials and development of research skills

Students can be introduced to different library research and reference materials by creating a worksheet requiring all students to investigate in different resources to obtain the required information. Publications such as: the *World Almanac* and *Information Please Almanac, Current Biography, The Negro Almanac*, and *The McGraw-Hill Encyclopedia of Science and Technology* are just a few of the books available in most library reference sections.

Consideration needs to be given to searching for information on the Internet also.

REFERENCE LIST

Au, K. H. 1993. *Literacy instruction in multicultural settings*. Orlando, FL.: Harcourt Brace.

------ 2002. Multicultural factors and effective instruction of students of diverse backgrounds. In A. Farstrup and S. J. Samuels (eds.) *What research says about reading Instruction* . Newark, DE: International Reading Assn. Coral Gables: U of Miami. 392-413.

Bebe, V.N & Mackey, W.F. *Bilingual schooling and the Miami experience.*

Berko Gleason, J. 1993. *The Development of Language* (3rd ed.) New York: Macmillan.

Bialystok, E. (ed.). 1991. *Language Processing in Bilingual Children*. Cambridge: CUP.

Burstall, C., Jamieson, M., Cohen, S. and Hargreaves, M. 1974. *Primary French I the balance*. Slough: NFER.

Candlin, C. 1987. In Batstone, R. 1994. *Grammar*. Oxford: OUP.

Chamot, A.U. and O'Malley, J. M. *The Calla Handbook*. Reading, MA: Addison-Wesley.

Collier, V.P. 1989. "How long? A synthesis of research on academic achievement in second language." *TESOL Quarterly*, 23. 509-531.

Collier, V. P. 1992. A synthesis of studies examining long-term language minority student data on academic achievement. *Bilingual Research Journal*, 16 (1-2). 187-212.

Collier, V. P. 1995. "Acquiring a second language for school." *Directions in Language & Education*. Washington, DC: NCBE. 1(4), 1-10.

Cummins, J. 1981. *Bilingualism and Minority Language Children*. Toronto: Institute for Studies in Education.

Diaz-Rico, L.T. and Weed, K.Z. 1995. *Language, and Academic Development Handbook: A Complete K-12 Reference Guide*. Needham Heights, MA: Allyn and Bacon.

Dulay, H. and Burt, M. 1974. "You can't learn without goofing" in J. Richards' (ed.) *Error Analysis, Perspectives on Second Language Acquisition*. New York: Longman.

Ellis, R. 1985. *Understanding Second Language Acquisition*. Oxford: OUP.

------ 1994. *The Study of Second Language Acquisition*. Oxford: OUP.

Entwhistle, N.J. and Entwhistle, D. 1970. The relationships between personality, study methods and academic performance. *British Journal of Educational Psychology.* Vol 40(2). doi.apa.org. 132-143.

Friend, M. and Bursuck, W. D. 2005. *Models of Coteaching: Including Students with Special Needs: A Practical Guide for Classroom Teachers.* (3rd ed.) Boston, MA: Allyn and Bacon.

Garcia, E. 1994. *Understanding and Meeting the Challenge of Student Cultural Diversity.* Boston: Houghton Mifflin.

Genesee, F. 1987. *Learning through Two Languages: Studies of Immersion and Bilingual Education.* Cambridge, MA: Newbury House.

------ (ed.) 1994. *Educating Second Language Children: The Whole Child, the Whole Curriculum, the Whole Community.* Cambridge: CUP.

Grellet, F. 1981. *Developing Reading Skills.* Cambridge: CUP.

Harris, M. and McCann, P. 1994. *Assessment.* Oxford: Heinemann.

Kramsch, C. 1998. *Language and Cullture.* Oxford: OUP.

Krashen, S. 1981. *Second Language Acquisition and Second Language Learning.* Oxford: Pergamon Press.

------1982. *Principles and Practice in Second Language Acquisition.* Oxford: Pergamon Press.

Lambert, W. and Klineberg, O. 1967. Children's views of foreign peoples: A crossnational study. New York: Appleton. (Review in Shumann, J., Affective factors and the problem of age in second language acquisition, *Language Learning* 25/2. 1975. 209-235).

Larsen, D. and Smalley, W. 1972. *Becoming Bilingual, a Guide to Language Learning.* New Canadian: CT. Practical Anthropology.

Larsen-Freeman, D. 1997. Chaos/complexity science and second language acquisition. *Applied Linguistics,*18 (2). 141-165.

Long, M. 1990. The lease a second language acquisition theory needs to explain. *TESOL Quarterly.* 24(4). 649-666.

McArthur, T. ed. 1992. *The Oxford Companion to the English Language.* Oxford: OUP. 571-573.

McClelland, D., Atkinson, J., Clark, R. & Lowell, E. 1953. *The Achievement Motive.* New York: Appleton, Century, Crofts.

McDonough, J. and Shaw, S. 1993. *Materials and Methods in ELT: A Teacher's Guide.* Blackwell.

McLaughlin, B. 1990.The development of bilingualism: Myth and reality. In A. Barona & E. Garcia (eds.) *Children at Risk: Poverty, Minority Status and other Issues in Educational Equity* . Washington, D.C.: National Association of School Psychologists. 65-76.

Naiman, N., Frolich, M., Stern, H., and Todesco, A. 1978. *The Good Language Learner.* Toronto: The Modern Language Centre, Ontario Institute for Studies in Education.

Nunan, D. 1989. *Designing Tasks for the Communicative Classroom.* Cambridge, CUP.

O'Malley, J. M. and Pierce, L. V. 1996. *Authentic Assessment for English Language Learners.* Longman.

Ovando, C.J., Coombs, M.C., and Collier, V.P. eds. 2006. *Bilingual and ESL Classrooms: Teaching in Multicultural Contexts* (4th ed.) Boston: McGraw-Hill.

Penfield, W. and Roberts, L. 1959. *Speech and Brain Mechanisms*. New York: Atheneum Press. (reviewed in Ellis, R. 1985).

Peregoy, S.F. and Boyle, O.F. 2008 *Reading, Writing, and Learning in ESL. 5th ed.* Boston: Pearson.

Prabhu, N. S. 1987. *Second Language Pedagogy: A Perspective.* London: Oxford, OUP.

Reid, J. The learning style preferences of ESL students. *TESOL Quarterly,* 21(1): 86-103.

Richards, Platt, and Weber. 1985. quoted by Ellis, R. The evaluation of communicative tasks in Tomlinson, B (ed.) *Materials Development in Language Teaching.* Cambridge: CUP. 1998.

Rosansky, E. The critical period for the acquisition of language: some cognitive developmental considerations. Working Papers on Bilingualism 6: 92-102.

Schmidt, R. W. 1990. The role of consciousness in second language acquisition. *Applied Linguistics,* 11(2). 129-158.

Schumm, J.S. 2006. *Reading Assessment and Instruction for All Learners*. New York: The Guilford Press.

Sinclair, J. and and Coulthard, M. 1975. Towards an Analysis of Discourse. Oxford: OUP. 93-94.

Slavin, R.E. and Cheung. 2003. *Effective Reading Programs for English Language Learners: A Best-Evidence Synthesis*. U.S. Dept. of Education. Institute of Education Sciences.

Snow, C. and Hoefnagel-Hohle, M. 1978. Age Differences in Second Language Learning. In *Second Language Acquisition,* Hatch ed. Rowley, MA.: Newbury House.

Teachers of English to Speakers of Other Languages. 1997. *ESL Standards for Pre-K— 12 Students.* Alexandria, VA.: TESOL.

Thomas, W. P., and Collier, V. P. 1995. Language minority student achievement and program effectiveness. Manuscript in preparation. (in Collier, V.P. 1995).

Traugott, E. C. and Pratt, M. L. 1980. *Linguistics for Students of Literature*. San Diego: Harcourt Brace Jovanovich.

Ur, P. 1996. *A Course in Language Teaching*. Cambridge: CUP.

Weir, C. 1993. *Understanding and Developing Language Tests*. Hemel Hempstead: Prentice Hall International.

Willing, K. 1988. "Learning strategies as information management: Some definitions for a theory of learning strategies". *Prospect* 3/2: 139-55.

Zwiers, J. 2007. *Building Academic Language. Essential Practices for Content Classrooms, Grades 5-12*. San Francisco: Jossey-Bass.

SAMPLE TEST

1. It is generally believed that language is ___:
(Easy) (Skill 1.1)

   A. Displaced.
   B. Culturally transmitted.
   C. Uniquely human.
   D. Not universal.

2. What was the single most important reason that English spread around the world?
(Average) (Skill 1.2)

   A. British colonialism.
   B. Settling of America.
   C. Spanish influence.
   D. Technology.

3. Which one of the following items is NOT an influence on how language grows naturally?
(Average) (Skill 1.3)

   A. Wars.
   B. Sports.
   C. Advertisers.
   D. Language societies.

4. The vocabulary word "ain't" has been used for /am not/, /is not/, and /has not/. It is an example of ____.
(Rigorous) (Skill 1.3)

   A. A dialect.
   B. How language evolves.
   C. Socio-economic effects on language.
   D. A southern drawl.

5. When a parent asks their child what they learned in school today, the child replies "Nothing," shrugging his or her shoulders. We have an example of ___.
(Average) (Skill 1.4)

   A. Morphology.
   B. Pragmatics.
   C. Syntax.
   D. Discourse.

6. Which of the following best illustrates the influence of culture, politics, or society on the speaker's choice of pragmatics?
(Rigorous) (Skill 1.5)

   A. A student approaches her friends and kisses them on the cheek.
   B. A student says "Hey, dude!" to his classmate.
   C. A student offers a "high five" to his classmates.
   D. Students from one country sit together and chatter in their native language.

7. **Which of the following best illustrates the lack of understanding of North American nonverbal cues and body language?**
(Rigorous) (Skill 1.6)

   A. Juan demonstrates how tall his sister is by holding his hand out with his palm down.

   B. Students from the European Union stand about one foot apart.

   C. Vietnamese students try to look the teacher in the eye even though they are uncomfortable doing so.

   D. Wu-Yuin never disagrees with statements made by the teacher, though he may challenge his classmates' statements.

8. **If you are studying phonology, you are studying:**
(Easy) (Skill 2.1)

   A. The smallest unit within a language system to which meaning is attached.

   B. The way in which speech sounds form patterns.

   C. Individual letters and letter combinations.

   D. The definition of individual words and sentences.

9. **"Bite" and "byte" are examples of which phonographemic differences?**
(Average) (Skill 2.1)

   A. Homonyms.
   B. Homographs.
   C. Homophones.
   D. Heteronyms.

10. **The study of morphemes may provide the student with:**
(Average) (Skill 2.2)

   A. The meaning of the root word.

   B. The meaning of the phonemes.

   C. Grammatical information.

   D. All of the above.

11. **If you are studying "syntax", you are studying:**
(Average) (Skill 2.3)

   A. Intonation and accent when conveying a message

   B. The rules for correct sentence structure.

   C. The definition of individual words and meanings.

   D. The subject-verb-object order of the English sentence.

12. **Language learners seem to acquire syntax:**
    (Average) (Skill 2.3)

    A. At the same rate in L1 and L2.
    B. Faster in L2 than L1.
    C. In the same order regardless of whether it is L1 or L2.
    D. In a different order for L1.

13. **Which one of the following is NOT included in the study of "semantics"?**
    (Rigorous) (Skill 2.4)

    A. Culture.
    B. The definition of individual words and meanings.
    C. The intonation of the speaker.
    D. Meaning which is "stored" or "inherent," as well as "contextual."

14. **Use the information below to answer the question that follows.**

    I'm a student from the island of Curacao. I'm happy that my country's soccer team is going to the FIFA World Cup. I'm excited because I've learned English for many years. Many people love to visit my country because of the beautiful beaches.

    Based on this writing sample, this student would likely benefit most from language instruction in which of the following areas?
    (Average) (Skill 2.5)

    A. Sentence formation, e.g., compound sentences and subordinate clauses.
    B. Cohesive devices, e.g., transitions and references to combine different parts of the text.
    C. Sentence mechanics, e.g., capitalization and punctuation.
    D. Verb tenses, e.g., present progressive and present perfect aspects.

15. **Respecting social diversity in the classroom means that teachers should teach standard English:**
(Easy) (Skill 2.6)

   A. Exclusively.
   B. While ignoring dialects.
   C. And explain the value of unique group variations as far as possible.
   D. While respecting and teaching awareness of unique group variations.

16. **Match the theorists with the elements of their explanations. (Place the letter after the number.)**
(Rigorous) (Skill 3.1)

   1. _____ **Chomsky**
   2. _____ **Piaget**
   3. _____ **Vygotsky**
   4. _____ **Collier**

   A. Children are active learners who construct their worlds.
   B. Social communication promotes language and cognition.
   C. Nature is more important than nurture.
   D. Language is a reflection of thought.

17. **The difference between learning a language and acquiring it is best illustrated by the example of:**
(Rigorous) (Skill 3.2)

   A. Studying the grammar of a language instead of learning it through reading, TV, etc.
   B. Children using language in play compared to an adult watching a movie.
   C. A child sounding out words and an adult helping the child with pronunciation.
   D. An immigrant trying to learn the language while at work, compared to a child learning the language at school.

18. **Which of the following periods of speech is being developed by the following activity?**
(Rigorous) (Skill 3.2)

Activity: The teacher tapes a short story of approximately 200-300 words to the wall at some distance from the students. She then divides the group into pairs. One student goes to the story and reads it. The first student (the runner) returns to his or her partner and dictates the story. Since it is unlikely that an ELL will remember the whole story exactly, the runner must make several trips.

A. Private speech.
B. Lexical chunks.
C. Experimental or simplified speech.
D. Formulaic speech.

19. **Which of the following does NOT illustrate the role of L1 on L2 learning?**
(Rigorous) (Skill 3.3)

A. High school students may do well orally, but be unable to understand written materials.
B. A gifted 5-year-old student is approximately halfway through his L1 language development.
C. An ELL who has not matured in his or her L1 has not acquired the subtleties of phonological distinctions.
D. Students who do not reach a certain level of knowledge in L1, including literacy, will have less difficulty acquiring a new language if it is introduced with L1.

20. An English Language Learner who has been living in the United States for many years is making little progress in her ESOL class. Her family and friends live in the same neighborhood as many of her relatives from her native land. Which one of the following conditions would probably have the most positive effect on the student's English language development?
(Rigorous) (Skill 3.4)

A. Reducing the time spent listening to and viewing media in the native language.
B. Decreasing the use of the native language in the home.
C. Adopting external elements of the U. S. culture such as music and clothing.
D. Increasing social contact with members of the U. S. culture.

21. Communication involves specific skills such as:
(Average) (Skill 3.5)

A. Turn-taking.
B. Silent period.
C. Lexical chunks.
D. Repetition.

22. Angela needs help in English. Her teacher suggested several things Angela can do to improve her learning strategies. One of the following is NOT a socioaffective learning strategy.
(Easy) (Skill 3.6)

A. Read a funny book.
B. Work cooperatively with her classmates.
C. Ask the teacher to speak more slowly.
D. Skim for information.

23. An ESOL teacher who encourages her students to keep track of their progress in English Language Learning is stimulating which learning strategy?
(Rigorous) (Skill 3.6)

A. Metacognitive.
B. Affective.
C. Cognitive.
D. Social.

24. Research shows that error correction in ELLs is a delicate business. Which of the following contributes to learning? Correction of:
(Rigorous) (Skill 3.7)

A. Semantic errors.
B. Grammatical errors.
C. Pronunciation.
D. All written work errors.

25. Which of the following approaches is based on using cognitive processes to solve problems?
(Rigorous) (Skill 4.1)

A. Total Physical Response.
B. Learning Experience Approach.
C. CALLA.
D. Gap activities.

26. Which of the following is NOT a manifestation of affective variables?
(Average) (Skill 4.2)

A. Anxiety.
B. Self-esteem.
C. Cognition.
D. Attitude.

27. Which of the following best describes 'facilitative' anxiety?
(Average) (Skill 4.2)

A. Juan always seems anxious and usually fails his tests.
B. Juanita hesitates to speak in front of her classmates.
C. Pedro looks worried all the time, but he usually does well on his tests.
D. Maria looks perplexed and seems lost in class. She cries a lot.

28. Which of the following factors is NOT a social factor affecting an ELL's language learning capabilities?
(Average) (Skill 4.3)

A. Gender.
B. Social class.
C. Age.
D. Level of English.

29. Which of the following indicates the learning style of an ELL who is interested in mathematics, can see planes in algebra, and can understand what an author means but does not specifically express?
(Rigorous) (Skill 4.4)

A. Concrete.
B. Analytic.
C. Communicative.
D. Authority-oriented.

30. **Which of the following statements is most accurate according to the latest research on learner variables?**
    (Rigorous) (Skill 4.4)

    A. Age determines when an ELL learns specific grammar points.
    B. The best language learners are young children.
    C. The most efficient language learners are teens.
    D. Teens learn to pronounce the language more accurately than adults or children.

31. **Interlanguage is best described as:**
    (Easy) (Skill 4.5)

    A. A language characterized by overgeneralization.
    B. Bilingualism.
    C. A language learning strategy.
    D. A strategy characterized by poor grammar.

32. **Upon arrival in a new country, immigrants frequently show signs of _____ in order to get a job.**
    (Easy) (Skill 5.1)

    A. Assimilation.
    B. Acculturation.
    C. Transculturation.
    D. Accommodation.

33. **Which of the following terms is the correct one for the situation below?**
    (Rigorous) (Skill 5.1)

    Situation: Ursula has lived in the U.S. for nearly five years. She rarely talks about her homeland and tries to imitate her classmates' speech and behavior. She is striving to be accepted by the culture surrounding her.

    A. Acculturation.
    B. Assimilation.
    C. Accommodation.
    D. Transculturation.

34. **Culture and cultural differences:**
    (Average) (Skill 5.2)

    A. Must be addressed by the teacher in the ELL classroom by pointing out cultural similarities and differences.
    B. Should be the starting point for learning about how culture affects the ELL's attitude towards education.
    C. Positively affects how well ELLs perform in the language classroom.
    D. May have strong emotional influence on the ELL learner.

35. Which of the following statements about culture and its manifestations is most likely to cause learning difficulties in the ELL?
(Average) (Skill 5.2)

A. Culture is synonymous with learning a language.
B. ELLs may not understand culture and its differences.
C. Teachers may offend students when they ignore cultural differences.
D. ELLs often believe their culture is superior to the one they are learning.

36. Which of the following cultural elements most likely explains the situation below?
(Easy) (Skill 5.3)

Situation: Amelia is conscientious in her studies, but she can't seem to finish on time, and gets angry when the teacher tells her to hand in her paper.

A. Family structure.
B. Roles and interpersonal relationships.
C. Discipline.
D. Time.

37. Pierre arrived in the U. S. in 2005. He has been living with his uncle and aunt who are well assimilated into the U.S. culture. Pierre misses his parents and brothers. He finds his high school studies fairly easy and his classmates lazy. He is worried about his goal of becoming a professional soccer player and doesn't understand why he can't have wine with his meals when he eats out with his aunt and uncle. In which stage of assimilation is Pierre?
(Average) (Skill 5.4)

A. Honeymoon stage.
B. Hostility stage.
C. Humor stage.
D. Home stage.

38. ESOL instruction frequently requires the teacher to change her instruction methods. One of the most difficult may be the:
(Rigorous) (Skill 5.5)

A. Wait time.
B. Establishment of group work.
C. Show and tell based on different cultures.
D. Extensive reading time.

39. **Which activity could be used to explore the cultural heritage of many diverse countries?**
    (Average) (Skill 6.1)

    A. Singing "Hava Nagila."
    B. Composing original parodies (e.g. "On Top of Spaghetti").
    C. Comparing proverbs from different countries.
    D. Writing Haiku poems.

40. **Which of the following best describes linguistic imperialism? The loss of native or heritage languages:**
    (Rigorous) (Skill 6.1)

    A. Due to the influence of other, dominant languages.
    B. Because of the Internet.
    C. Because of the globalization of goods and trade.
    D. Due to the limited resources of the native or heritage culture.

41. **Which of the following relationships would probably cause the least conflict for an immigrant in the U. S.?**
    (Average) (Skill 6.2)

    A. School.
    B. Religious beliefs.
    C. Workplace relationships.
    D. Desire for better status for future.

42. **Which of the following is NOT a method for discovering a person's height in English speaking cultures?**
    (Easy) (Skill 6.4)

    A. Measuring another's height by comparing shoulder heights.
    B. Measuring two people back-to-back.
    C. Stating a person is almost as tall as someone else.
    D. Holding the hand out with the thumb pointing upward.

43. **Which of the following strategies provides the ELL with the opportunity to celebrate his/her native culture and the U.S. culture at the same time?**
    (Rigorous) (Skill 6.4)

    A. ELL-created role plays highlighting common cultural misunderstandings.
    B. a telephone conversation between a foreign customer and a U.S. company read from a textbook.
    C. A learning diary about the ELL's difficulties in English.
    D. Teacher-assigned research on different cultures.

44. **Which of the following statements are examples of stereotyping? (You may choose more than one.) (Rigorous) (Skill 7.3)**

   A. All U.S. citizens are educated.
   B. All Latinos can dance.
   C. All Europeans speak several languages.
   D. All of the above.

45. **The decision by which the U.S. Supreme Court essentially mandated bilingual instruction was: (Easy) (Skill 7.1)**

   A. The Civil Rights Act.
   B. Lau v. Nichols.
   C. Castaneda v. Pickard.
   D. No Child Left Behind.

46. **The No Child Left Behind Act established that: (Rigorous) (Skill 7.1)**

   A. Title I funds are available only if the schools participate in National Assessment of Education Progress.
   B. Bilingual programs must be effective within three specific criteria.
   C. High performance children cannot be used to average out low-performing ELLs.
   D. Schools must form and convene assessment committees.

47. **In contrast to many state positions, the federal government advocates ____ for ELLs: (Average) (Skill 7.1)**

   A. Higher funding for inner-city schools.
   B. Equal opportunities and protection.
   C. Restructuring of school districts.
   D. A technologically prepared workforce.

48. **In schools with large immigrant populations of diverse origin, the most commonly used model is: (Average) (Skill 7.2)**

   A. Submersion.
   B. Pull-out ESL.
   C. SDAIE.
   D. Transition.

49. **CALLA is an example of which of the following models used to instruct ELLs? (Average) (Skill 7.2)**

   A. Structured English immersion.
   B. Communication-based ESL.
   C. Submersion with primary language support.
   D. Content-based ESL.

50. **Which of the following is one of the goals of the International Baccalaureate Program?**
(Rigorous) (Skill 7.3)

A. Promote the teaching of English abroad.
B. Encourage foreign students to learn English well.
C. Permit foreign students to study English as native speakers do.
D. Standardize content areas in schools of diverse countries.

51. **Which of the following is a key element in professional development?**
(Average) (Skill 7.4)

A. Consulting a mentor.
B. Creating a portfolio.
C. Joining professional support groups, (e.g., TESOL).
D. Planning and writing down goals.

52. **Which of the following is NOT the role of the ESOL resource person?**
(Average) (Skill 7.5)

A. Encouraging a text-rich environment.
B. Maintaining an ample supply of realia.
C. Conducting workshops on discourse analysis.
D. Reporting a suspected case of child abuse.

53. **Homeroom teacher A enjoys teaching literature while homeroom teacher B enjoys teaching mathematics. Which of the following teaching models might best accommodate their preferences?**
(Rigorous) (Skill 7.6)

A. One teach, one assist.
B. Parallel teaching.
C. Team teaching.
D. One teach, one observe.

54. **A newly immigrated family has expressed the desire to mingle with native-speaking Americans in order to polish their English speaking skills. Which one of the following actions would probably be the most appropriate and effective in addressing the mother's and father's needs to mingle with native-speaking Americans?**
(Easy) (Skill 8.1)

A. Suggest a private class in their home.
B. Provide literature about the programs offered at the local mall for diet and exercise.
C. Mention the YMCA/YWCA and their services.
D. Recommend the public library and its adult programs.

55. An English Language Learner who is a recent immigrant to the United States has been given a placement test and placed in the intermediate ESOL level. She is in high school and her other test results suggest an advanced placement in biology which she claims to really like. The science teacher is reluctant to accept her in his class because of her English level. He is worried that she will be unable to understand the course materials. Which of the following approaches would be the most effective for the ESOL teacher to use to help the student?
(Average) (Skill 8.2)

A. Offering to work closely with the biology teacher to provide the ELL with the English language support she needs to take the advanced course.

B. Suggesting the student take a lower level science course until her language skills test at the advanced level.

C. Asking the biology teacher to provide advanced-level biology materials that the ESOL teacher could include in the ELL's language instruction.

D. Recommending that the student focus on developing her English language skills before attempting advanced content coursework.

56. The teacher of an eighth-grade class in public school ABC has six Asian, and three Latino ELLs with very low English skills. Each student is from a different country. Which of the following educational models would probably serve the ELLs best?
(Average) (Skill 8.2)

A. Pull-out model.
B. Resource center/lab.
C. Cluster center.
D. Scheduled class period only.

57. Which of the following is a software translating program that could be helpful to ELLs?
(Rigorous) (Skill 8.3)

A. SimCity.
B. Fast ForWord.
C. Babel Fish.
D. Content Mania.

58. Which point is the aim of the 2009 version of the Dream Act?
(Rigorous) (Skill 8.4)

A. Promote military service or college education of older illegal immigrants.
B. Permit children who immigrated to the U.S. at an early age to acquire legal status independently of their parents.
C. Encourage good moral character from undocumented immigrants.
D. Advocate education for legal aliens.

59. The school is planning a "Grandparents Day." Which of the following activities could be best used to promote the ESOL program?
(Easy) (Skill 8.5)

A. A bake sale.
B. Sports activities, (e.g., yoga, soccer, etc.).
C. Skits by children.
D. Simple board games incorporating ESOL techniques in the game.

60. Based on the last two years' test scores, school XYZ has ranked near the bottom in the district. Which of the following strategies would be most appropriate for involving the community in turning the school around?
(Easy) (Skill 8.6)

A. A series of lectures and newsletters in the native language of the students.
B. Increased security.
C. Involving the older members of the community in mentoring or tutoring programs.
D. Inviting high profile sports figures to speak on the value of education.

61. An ELL in middle school has been in the United States for two years but has recently been transferred to a new school. He seems to do well in most classes, but has difficulties in math. What would be the most appropriate strategy to help him learn the content-related material?
(Rigorous) (Skill 9.1)

A. Provide intensive vocabulary instruction on the relevant material.
B. Activate background knowledge.
C. Explain the concepts in his native language.
D. Arrange for a pull-out period with other ELLs.

62. Advanced TPR might include:
(Easy) (Skill 9.2)

A. Rapid fire commands.
B. More advanced vocabulary.
C. Funny commands.
D. All of the above.

63. Which of the following best describes the goal of CALLA?
(Easy) (Skill 9.2)

A. Active learning in the regular classroom.
B. Full participation in ESOL classes.
C. Math studies for advanced ELLs.
D. Transition from ESOL language programs to regular classroom programs.

64. Which of the following instructional approaches emphasizes LEPs working on content?
(Average) (Skill 9.2)

A. TPR.
B. The Natural Approach.
C. CALLA.
D. The Communicative Approach.

65. A parent filled out the home language survey as indicated below:

Is a language other than English used in the home?
-Yes.

Does the student have a first language other than English?
-Yes.

Does the student most frequently speak a language other than English?
-No.

What is the school's next step?
(Rigorous) (Skill 9.3)

A. Placing the student at grade level with no assessment.
B. Postponing admission until testing is completed.
C. Assigning the student to an ESOL program while beginning testing.
D. Placing the student in the grade-level ESOL program.

66. **Which of the following options is best for the ESOL teacher to use to activate background knowledge? (Average) (Skill 9.3)**

A. Demonstrating using realia.
B. Asking questions about the topic using a picture to illustrate the topic.
C. Reading the text with the ELL and explaining as you go.
D. Allowing the ELL to watch a video on the school intranet.

67. **The 5th grade content area teacher has decided to use stories in her classroom for all students. What would be the best strategy to use so that the ELLs also participate? (Rigorous) (Skill 9.4)**

A. Discuss favorite stories with the class.
B. Bring in picture books of children's stories.
C. Have children draw their own stories.
D. Group the students together and have them retell their favorite movies.

68. **Which of the following is the best option for introducing new vocabulary to pre-literate ELLs? (Easy) (Skill 9.4)**

A. Wall charts.
B. Word ladders.
C. Stories.
D. Spelling lists.

69. **Which of the following best illustrates how ESOL teachers can help all their ELLs feel the classroom is a safe, welcoming environment? (Rigorous) (Skill 9.5)**

A. Learning corners are set up around the room for free exploration.
B. The ESOL area is a rich environment with materials about the ELL's homeland.
C. A companion is assigned to each ELL to help them learn where things are and what to do in social situations.
D. The ESOL instructor corrects the ELL's oral language and keeps track of the errors they commit.

70. **Which is the best option to improve ELLs' English language skills overall? (Rigorous) (Skill 9.6)**

   A. Students report on something familiar to them such as their home country or a friend.
   B. Choral recitation of dialogs.
   C. Practice in writing dictated passages.
   D. Drills using TPR.

71. **An ESOL teacher wants to have her ELLs work in small groups. Which of the following techniques/resources would provide the best support to the students? (Rigorous) (Skill 9.7)**

   A. Internet research facilities.
   B. Library access.
   C. Bilingual dictionaries.
   D. Interactive scaffolding.

72. **The content area teacher wants the class to write as part of a unit on mammals. Which activity would be the most challenging way to test learning while incorporating other language skills in the activity? (Rigorous) (Skill 9.8)**

   A. A summary of a written text in a graphic form.
   B. A drawing with a short paragraph explaining the drawing.
   C. A letter to the editor of the daily paper.
   D. A dialogue between two animals.

73. **Which of the following would be the best option for an authentic response to the topic of endangered species? (Rigorous) (Skill 9.8)**

   A. Draw your favorite endangered animal and explain why it is your favorite.
   B. Write a dialogue between two people discussing the problems associated with endangered animals.
   C. Write a letter to the magazine of the Sierra Club.
   D. Write a journal entry expressing your personal feelings.

74. Which one of the following kinds of text is NOT user-friendly for beginning readers?
(Rigorous) (Skill 10.1)

Texts which:

A. Summarize key points.
B. Have highlighted vocabulary.
C. Use advanced vocabulary.
D. Contain new vocabulary.

75. When using concept maps, the students must learn to ___ the different elements of the topic.
(Average) (Skill 10.1)

A. Rank.
B. Organize.
C. Evaluate.
D. Associate.

76. When an ESOL teacher is helping an ELL to understand difficult material, which of the following theorist's principals is the teacher implementing?
(Rigorous) (Skill 10.2)

A. Cummins.
B. Vygotsky.
C. Tompkins.
D. Krashen.

77. Which of the following operations is the ESOL teacher using when she teaches the concept of "mother/madre/mere"?
(Rigorous) (Skill 10.3)

A. Cognates.
B. Nominalization.
C. Vocabulary.
D. Idioms.

78. When teaching ELLs the same content as mainstream students, but using different types of resources, the ESOL teacher is helping the ELLs in which of the following ways?
(Rigorous) (Skill 10.3)

A. By creating different learning goals.
B. By appealing to the different senses.
C. By recognizing and using different intelligences.
D. By employing different learning styles.

79. Which is NOT a category of the K-W-L chart?
(Easy) (Skill 10.4)

A. List what you want to know.
B. List what you learned.
C. List what you must learn.
D. List what you know.

80. **When considering using technology in the classroom, which of the following criteria is most important for the ESOL teacher keep in mind? (Rigorous) (Skill 10.5)**

    A. Is the technology (e.g., the Internet) the most efficient method of teaching the material?
    B. Is the project designed with the learner in mind?
    C. Will you be able to communicate by Internet with each student personally at least once a month?
    D. Will this project contribute to the ELL's learning portfolio?

81. **Which of the following is NOT an acceptable alternative assessment strategy for ELLs? (Average) (Skill 11.1)**

    A. Portfolios.
    B. Observation.
    C. Self-assessment.
    D. Essay writing.

82. **Which of the following is the most appropriate method for aligning instruction with assessment? (Average) (Skill 11.2)**

    A. The ESOL instructor teaches the students from their "needs" level.
    B. The content area instructor fully informs the ESOL instructor of the curriculum requirements.
    C. The content area teacher provides vocabulary lists to the ESOL instructor.
    D. The ESOL teacher instructs the ELLs in content area materials based on their needs.

83. **When testing for an ELL's level of English proficiency, which minor accommodation is appropriate? (Rigorous) (Skill 11.3)**

    A. Allowing extra time if necessary.
    B. Using the ELL's portfolio.
    C. Recitation.
    D. Providing translation of prompts as needed for understanding.

84. **Which of the following characteristics may indicate an ELL who is gifted? (Average) (Skill 11.3)**

   A. Learns content well but has some language difficulties.
   B. Able to solve problems independently of the language (e.g., math problems).
   C. Good learner in heritage language.
   D. Good academic history from native land.

85. **Which of the following tests is represented in the following example?**

   Example: Students are required to listen to an announcement in a train station and fill in a chart. (Rigorous) (Skill 11.5)

   A. Traditional tests.
   B. Criterion-referenced tests.
   C. Norm-referenced tests.
   D. Third generation tests.

86. **Before coming to the U.S., Sven, an 11th-grade student, took the TOEFL. This is a _____ test. (Easy) (Skill 11.6)**

   A. Language proficiency.
   B. Language achievement.
   C. Language placement.
   D. Diagnostic language.

87. **Which of the following tests is an example of language achievement tests? (Average) (Skill 11.6)**

   A. A final exam.
   B. Foreign Service Exam (FSI).
   C. A placement test.
   D. Test of Spoken English (TSE)

88. **Which of the following statements is NOT correct? (Average) (Skill 11.7)**

   A. All ELLs are required to participate in all assessment programs.
   B. All ELLs are allowed to defer assessment for one year.
   C. WIDA tests ELLs' language skills in all four language domains.
   D. Ending special services is usually based on a combination of performance criteria.

89. **Which method is the most appropriate for dealing partially with cultural bias in tests? (Rigorous) (Skill 11.8)**

   A. Translate the tests previous to the actual exam.
   B. Provide pictures and graphics during the test.
   C. Administer practice tests with time limits.
   D. Provide a study guide and give test orally.

90. Which of the following test attributes is questioned when assessing an ELL's writing journal? (Rigorous) (Skill 11.8)

   A. Practicality.
   B. Reliability.
   C. Concurrent validity.
   D. Predictive validity.

91. What is the primary goal of the Georgia Alternate Assessment test? (Average) (Skill 12.1)

   A. Provide ELLs in gifted programs access to more challenging curriculum.
   B. Administer a test to determine the placement of ELLs.
   C. Ensure all individuals access to the curriculum of the State of Georgia.
   D. Ensure all ELLs classified as individuals with disabilities an education.

92. Which of the following statements is NOT a valid reason for administering self-assessment tests? (Average) (Skill 12.2)

   A. It relieves the burden of assessment on the teacher.
   B. It provides useful information.
   C. It illustrates ELLs' feelings about their grades.
   D. It develops self-directed language learners.

93. Which of the following criteria should NOT be included in an oral evaluation of ELLs? (Average) (Skill 12.3)

   A. Reading a dialogue.
   B. Accuracy.
   C. Telling a story.
   D. Asking for clarification.

94. Which of the following tasks is a valid reading evaluation of ELLs? (Average) (Skill 12.4)

   A. Multiple choice questions.
   B. Open-ended questions.
   C. Completing a text with information based on class work.
   D. Information transfer.

95. Which of the following tasks could be included in a writing evaluation of ELLs? (Average) (Skill 12.5)

   A. Multiple choice questions.
   B. Reading a dialogue and answering questions.
   C. Responding to information given.
   D. Cloze summaries.

96. Which of the following methods could be used to evaluate ELLs in content area material? (Average) (Skill 12.6)

   A. Multiple choice.
   B. True-false.
   C. Essays.
   D. Exhibits or projects.

97. **Which of the following activities would encourage authentic oral language production in ELLs?**
(Average) (Skill 13.1)

   A. Group work.
   B. Oral quizzes.
   C. One-on-one interviews with the teacher.
   D. Oral reports.

98. **Which of the following activities is probably the most meaningful for developing ELL's communicative skills?**
(Rigorous) (Skill 13.2)

   A. Cloze procedure activities.
   B. Gap-filling activities.
   C. Role plays and skits.
   D. TPR.

99. **Which of the following instructions is appropriate for introducing a listening exercise to ELLs?**
(Average) (Skill 13.3)

   A. Introducing the dialog with "Listen to the passage…".
   B. Presenting a speaker by stating his name and to whom he is related to in the class.
   C. Stating the context of the passage being presented.
   D. Assigning five questions to be answered during the listening process by stating that they are a quiz.

100. **Which one of the following activities would be the best option for teaching stress in speech?**
(Easy) (Skill 13.4)

   A. Have students listen to a text being read and follow the stress patterns marked in the textbook.
   B. Have students beat out the rhythm while listening to a text.
   C. Have students silently read a text and mark the stressed words.
   D. Explain the rules for stress in words and sentences in English.

101. **When the teacher is correcting a student's speech, the teacher should:**
(Easy) (Skill 13.4)

   A. Carefully correct all mistakes.
   B. Consider the context of the error.
   C. Confirm the error by repeating it.
   D. Repeat the student's message but correcting it.

102. **Which of the following types of correction is appropriate?**
(Easy) (Skill 14.1)

   A. Lexical correction.
   B. Correcting sentence semantic errors.
   C. Pragmatic correction.
   D. Correction of simplification errors.

103. **When correcting written work, what is the most effective way for the teacher to correct the paper of her ELLs?**
(Easy) (Skill 14.1)

    A. Correct all vocabulary errors.
    B. Correct some grammatical errors.
    C. Correct all errors.
    D. Correct one example of different types of errors.

104. **Which of the following options is probably the most beneficial to ELLs who do not yet read in their native language?**
(Easy) (Skill 14.2)

    A. Instruction based on needs.
    B. Involving the ELL's family.
    C. Oral storytelling in the classroom.
    D. Using the same methods of instruction as used for native speakers.

105. **Which of the following ESL goals is achieved when having ELLs retell a story?**
(Easy) (Skill 14.3)

    A. ELLs are better able to understand the culture of the story.
    B. ELLs obtain practice in recognizing the important story elements.
    C. ELLs are able to incorporate some of the language of the story in their speech.
    D. ELLs derive esthetic pleasure from the story.

106. **What is the best option for beginning reading instruction for ELLs who have reached the level of speech emergence in their native language?**
(Average) (Skill 14.4)

    A. Reading instruction should be delayed until the ELL has mastered the oral language of his native language.
    B. Reading instruction should be begun after one year in the U.S. school system where the ELL received oral English language instruction.
    C. Reading instruction should be begun in the ELL's L1.
    D. All ELLs benefit from beginning reading instruction in L2.

107. **Which of the following writing traits are illustrated in the passage which follows?**
(Rigorous) (Skill 14.5)

Writing passage: "My country is beautiful. I love my country very much. My mother love my country. She is sad to leave and come U.S."

A. Fluency: Beginning Level, Sentence Variety: Beginning Level.
B. Fluency: Intermediate Level, Vocabulary: Intermediate Level.
C. Grammar: Beginning Level, Organization: Intermediate Level.
D. Grammar: Intermediate Level, Genre: Intermediate Level.

108. **Which one of the following is a negative result of instructing children in their first language?**
(Average) (Skill 15.1)

A. Instruction in L1 lowers the affective filter.
B. L1 instruction clarifies misunderstandings in L2.
C. L1 instruction can be used to explain differences between L1 and L2.
D. ELLs can become dependent upon L1 instruction.

109. **Which one of the following is NOT a step in the Language Experience Approach?**
(Average) (Skill 15.2)

A. The ELL retells a personal story.
B. While writing the story down, the teacher makes minor grammar corrections.
C. The ELL reads his or her story.
D. The students illustrate or dramatize the story.

110. **Which one of the following does NOT represent a beginning reading development technique?**
(Average) (Skill 15.3)

A. Holding up the left hand in order to remember which side of the text to begin reading first.
B. Memorizing sight words.
C. Learning sentence structure patterns.
D. Memorizing vocabulary lists.

111. **Which of the following is NOT a reading comprehension skill?**
(Average) (Skill 15.4)

A. Skimming.
B. Scanning.
C. Restating.
D. Describing.

112. Which of the following is NOT an academic writing skill?
(Average) (Skill 15.5)

A. Planning the paper.
B. Doing research.
C. Quick-writing the paper.
D. Revising.

113. Which of the following is an important skill that ELLs entering the U.S. school system in middle or high school will probably not possess even if they are fairly skilled in academic writing?
(Average) (Skill 15.6)

A. Using dictionaries.
B. Using advanced vocabulary.
C. Writing in different genres.
D. Using connectors.

114. When addressing school-age ELLs who do not read in their heritage language, which one of the following is the LEAST appropriate action?
(Rigorous) (Skill 16.1)

A. Introducing topics such as life survival skills.
B. Having them read authentic materials such as menus.
C. Using the Language Experience Approach.
D. Using CALLA.

115. Which one of the following is the LEAST appropriate strategy for activating prior knowledge and relating it to the content-area objectives in the English classroom?
(Rigorous) (Skill 16.2)

A. Creating "All about Me" autobiographies.
B. Using dialogue journals.
C. Discussing themes such as "Family Origins".
D. Having Q and A sessions with the ELLs about home culture.

116. Which one of the following is NOT the most appropriate option to make content-area lessons accessible to ELLs?
(Easy) (Skill 16.3)

A. Using vocabulary lists from the text.
B. Speaking loudly so that they understand.
C. Reading the story/text and checking for comprehension constantly.
D. Writing new vocabulary words, expressions or idioms on the white board.

117. **When bringing ELLs up to grade level, which of the following is the most appropriate option for the ESOL teacher? (Rigorous) (Skill 16.4)**

A. Teach according to curriculum.
B. Select high-priority concepts for instruction.
C. Instruct the ELL in appropriate language skills.
D. Concentrate on pronunciation and listening skills.

118. **Which one of the following is NOT a tenet of CALLA? (Rigorous) (Skill 16.5)**

A. In mathematics, science, etc., grade level should determine content.
B. ELLs can gradually learn the specific language of the subject area.
C. Encourage ELLs to use higher level cognitive processes.
D. Reading in L2 can be postponed until oral language is developed.

119. **Which of the following options is NOT a cognitive-learning strategy? (Rigorous) (Skill 16.6)**

A. Note-taking.
B. Ordering.
C. K-W-L charts.
D. Classifying.

120. **Which of the following options would best serve ELLs in learning about the library? (Average) (Skill 16.7)**

A. A tour and introduction by the librarian.
B. A text on the library followed by comprehension exercises.
C. A gap-filling exercise on the library.
D. A quiz on the library.

CONSTRUCTED RESPONSE   **ASSIGNMENT ONE**

Use the information below to complete the assignment that follows.

Developing knowledge and skills in English semantics is an essential component of learning English as a new language.

- Describe one instructional strategy that an ESOL teacher could use to promote an English Language Learner's development of knowledge and skills in English semantics.

- Explain why the strategy would be effective in the development of English as a new language.

RESPONSE SHEET FOR CONSTRUCTED RESPONSE ASSIGNMENT ONE

CONSTRUCTED RESPONSE   **ASSIGNMENT TWO**

Use the information below to complete the assignment that follows.

The process of culture shock can be difficult for most English Language Learning students.

- Describe one strategy an ESOL instructor can use to support the ELL in the process of culture shock; and

- Explain why the strategy would be effective.

RESPONSE SHEET FOR CONSTRUCTED RESPONSE ASSIGNMENT TWO

CONSTRUCTED RESPONSE   **ASSIGNMENT THREE**

Use the information below to complete the assignment that follows.

There is a variety of instructional methodologies and approaches ESOL teachers can use to assess the English Language Learner's progress in English besides standardized testing.

- Describe one instructional setting (i.e. individual student, small group, or whole class), including language-proficiency level of student(s), and a situation in which it would be appropriate for an ESOL teacher to use an alternative assessment;

- Explain why this alternative assessment would be an effective way to assess the ELL. Be sure to include information about specific features of the assessment and its characteristics or goals to support your explanation.

RESPONSE SHEET FOR CONSTRUCTED RESPONSE ASSIGNMENT THREE

CONSTRUCTED RESPONSE   **ASSIGNMENT FOUR**

Use the information below to complete the assignment that follows.

ESOL teachers use a variety of strategies to promote English Language Learners' written language development.

- Describe one instructional strategy that an ESOL teacher could use to promote an English Language Learner's development of writing academic papers in science.

- Explain why the strategy you described would be effective in developing the ELL's academic writing.

RESPONSE SHEET FOR CONSTRUCTED RESPONSE ASSIGNMENT FOUR

Answer Key

1. C	45. B	89. C
2. A	46. C	90. A
3. D	47. B	91. C
4. B	48. B	92. C
5. B	49. D	93. A
6. A	50. D	94. D
7. D	51. D	95. C
8. A	52. D	96. D
9. C	53. C	97. A
10. C	54. D	98. C
11. B	55. A	99. C
12. C	56. B	100. B
13. A	57. C	101. D
14. B	58. B	102. A
15. D	59. D	103. D
16. –	60. C	104. A
17. A	61. A	105. C
18. B	62. D	106. D
19. D	63. D	107. A
20. D	64. C	108. D
21. A	65. C	109. B
22. D	66. A	110. D
23. A	67. D	111. D
24. A	68. C	112. C
25. D	69. C	113. C
26. C	70. A	114. B
27. C	71. D	115. D
28. D	72. A	116. B
29. B	73. C	117. B
30. C	74. C	118. D
31. C	75. A	119. A
32. D	76. D	120. C
33. B	77. A	
34. D	78. C	
35. C	79. C	
36. D	80. A	
37. B	81. D	
38. A	82. B	
39. C	83. A	
40. A	84. B	
41. D	85. D	
42. D	86. A	
43. A	87. A	
44. –	88. B	

Rationales

1. **It is generally believed that language is ___:**
   (Easy) (Skill 1.1)

   A. Displaced.
   B. Culturally transmitted.
   C. Uniquely human.
   D. Not universal.

   Answer: C. Uniquely human

   Many linguists believe that language is a defining characteristic of the human species, and one which distinguishes humans from others of the animal kingdom. Humans' system of communication can be used in other media such as writing, print, and physical signs.

2. **What was the single most important reason that English spread around the world?**
   (Average) (Skill 1.2)

   A. British colonialism.
   B. Settling of America.
   C. Spanish influence.
   D. Technology.

   Answer: A. British colonialism.

   As the British expanded their empire, their language spread all over the world as well. The sun never set on the British Empire during the 19th century. In many of these countries, English has become an official language. (The predominance of English in data banks—an estimated 80-90 percent of the world's data banks are in English—keeps English the foremost language in the world today.)

3. Which one of the following items is NOT a cause of language growing naturally?
   (Average) (Skill 1.3)

   A. Wars
   B. Sports
   C. Advertisers
   D. Language societies

   Answer: D. Language societies.

   While options A, B, and C have promoted the growth of English, language societies (D) are a limiting factor. Their primary concern is the "purity" of the language which they govern. Instead of allowing the growth of the language by creating new words, they limit the language by insisting that old words are recycled to meet the demands of modern society.

4. The vocabulary word "ain't" has been used for /am not/, /is not/, and /has not/. It is an example of _____ .
   (Rigorous) (Skill 1.3)

   A. A dialect.
   B. How language evolves.
   C. Socio-economic effects on language.
   D. A southern drawl.

   Answer: B. How language evolves.

   The word "ain't" first came into usage in the 17th century when many different contracted forms of speech began to appear. For reasons unknown, in the U.S. it became unacceptable (as did many other contracted forms), but remains in regular usage in rural, working class, and inner city people's speech. In the 17th century it was used instead of has not/have not (*an't/ain't*); in the 18th century /an't/ was used for *am not, are not,* and *is not.* It is an excellent example of B-- how language evolves.

5. **When a parent asks their child what they learned in school today and the child replies 'Nothing' shrugging his or her shoulders, we have an example of ___.**
(Average) (Skill 1.4)

A. Morphology.
B. Pragmatics.
C. Syntax.
D. Discourse.

Answer: B. Pragmatics.

Pragmatics is the study of how context impacts the interpretation of the language. Parents and children are following a well-scripted situation in which the parent is showing concern about the child's education, and the child is resisting. The child is probably more interested in relaxing, playing with toys, watching TV, or anything else but reliving what went on in the classroom. What's more, it's difficult to explain what was actually learned if it was only introduced and the class will probably spend many more days on the topic.

6. **Which of the following best illustrates the influence of culture, politics, or society on the speaker's choice of pragmatics?**
(Rigorous) (Skill 1.5)

A. A student approaches her friends and kisses them on the cheek.
B. A student says "Hey, dude!" to his classmate.
C. A student offers a "high five" to his classmates.
D. Students from one country sit together and chatter in their native language.

Answer: A. A student approaches her friends and kisses them on the cheek.

In options B and C, the students are trying to assimilate into the new culture. In D, the students are relaxing and chattering as if they would if they if they were in their native land. Thus, a student who approaches her friends and kisses them on the cheek is demonstrating a cultural behavior from her native land.

7. Which of the following best illustrates the lack of understanding of North American nonverbal cues and body language?
(Rigorous) (Skill 1.6)

    A. Juan demonstrates how tall his sister is by holding his hand out with his palm down.
    B. Students from the European Union stand about one foot apart.
    C. Vietnamese students try to look at the teacher in the eye even though they are uncomfortable doing so.
    D. Wu-Yuin never disagrees with statements made by the teacher, but he may challenge his classmates' statements.

Answer: D. Wu-Yuin never disagrees with statements made by the teacher, but he may challenge his classmates' statements.

Options A, B, and C demonstrate behavior that is indicative of students trying to assimilate the culture mores of the United States. Only option D illustrates a student who may be having difficulties assimilating the North American culture. Asian students typically respect their elders and do not challenge them either by asking questions or disagreeing with them.

8. If you are studying phonology, then you are studying:
(Easy) (Skill 2.1)

    A. The smallest unit within a language system, to which meaning is attached.
    B. The way in which speech sounds form patterns.
    C.   Individual letters and letter combinations.
    D. The definition of individual words and sentences.

Answer: B. The way in which speech sounds form patterns.

The smallest unit within a language system to which meaning is attached is a morpheme. The term *phonographemic* refers to the study of individual letters and letter combinations. The definition of individual words is known as making the meaning of a word explicit. The way in which speech sounds form patterns is phonology, so option B the best answer.

9. "Bite" and "byte" are examples of which phonographemic differences? (Average) (Skill 2.1)

   A. Homonyms.
   B. Homographs.
   C. Homophones.
   D. Heteronyms.

   Answer: C. Homophones.

   "Homonyms" is a general term for words with two or more meanings. Homographs are two or more words with the same spelling or pronunciation, but different meanings. Heteronyms are two or more words that have the same spelling but different meanings and spellings. Homophones are words that have the same pronunciation, but different meanings and spellings. D is the correct response.

10. The study of morphemes may provide the student with: (Average) (Skill 2.2)

    A. The meaning of the root word.
    B. The meaning of the phonemes.
    C. Grammatical information.
    D. All of the above.

    Answer: C. Grammatical information.

    The meaning of the root word comes from its source or origin, and the meaning of phonemes relates to its sound. The correct answer is C which gives grammatical information to the student (e.g., prepositions or articles).

**11. If you are studying "syntax", you are studying:
(Average) (Skill 2.3)**

    A. Intonation and accent when conveying a message.
    B. The rules for correct sentence structure.
    C. The definition of individual words and meanings.
    D. The subject-verb-object order of the English sentence.

Answer: B. The rules for correct sentence structure.

The intonation and accent used when conveying a message refer to pitch and stress. The definition of individual words and meanings is semantics. The subject-verb-object order of the English sentence refers to is the correct order for most English sentences, but the rules for correct sentence structure comprise syntax, so B is the best option.

**12. Language learners seem to acquire syntax:
(Average) (Skill 2.3)**

    A. At the same rate in L1 and L2.
    B. Faster in L2 than L1.
    C. In the same order regardless of whether it is L1 or L2.
    D. In a different order for L1.

Answer: C. In the same order regardless of whether it is in L1 or L2.

All language learners must progress through the same hierarchical steps in their language learning process. They go from the least to the most complicated stages, regardless of whether it is in L1 or L2.

**13. Which one of the following is NOT included in the study of "semantics"?
(Rigorous) (Skill 2.4)**

    A. Culture.
    B. The definition of individual words and meanings.
    C. The intonation of the speaker.
    D. Meaning which is "stored" or "inherent", as well as "contextual".

Answer: A. Culture.

Since semantics refers to the definition of individual words and meanings, the intonation of the speaker, and meaning which is "stored" or "inherent", as well as "contextual", option A is the best response.

14. Use the information below to answer the question that follows.

I'm a student from the island of Curacao. I'm happy that my country's soccer team is going to the FIFA World Cup. I'm excited because I've learned English for many years. Many people love to visit my country because of the beautiful beaches.

Based on this writing sample, this student would likely benefit most from language instruction in which of the following areas?
(Average) (Skill 2.5)

A. Sentence formation, e.g., compound sentences and subordinate clauses
B. Cohesive devices, e.g., transitions and references to combine different parts of the text.
C. Sentence mechanics, e.g. capitalization and punctuation.
D. Verb tenses, e.g., present progressive and present perfect aspects.

Answer: B. Cohesive devices, e.g., transitions, and references to combine different parts of the text

This ELL's problem is in paragraph cohesion. To make smooth transitions between ideas and subjects in a paragraph, the ELL needs to use cohesive devices such as linking expressions (e.g., by the way, what I am trying to say, etc.) and connectors (e.g., and, but, too, nevertheless). By learning to use these devices, the ELL will soon learn to eliminate unrelated statements or to create a new paragraph.

15. Respecting social diversity in the classroom means that teachers should teach standard English:
(Easy) (Skill 2.6)

A. Exclusively.
B. While ignoring dialects.
C. And explain the value of unique group variations as far as possible.
D. While respecting and teaching awareness of unique group variations.

Answer: D. While respecting and teaching awareness of unique group variations.

In the modern world, English is being seen more and more as a "world language" used by many peoples who are not from the traditional English- speaking countries: Great Britain, the United States, Canada, Australia, etc. This has caused theorists to suggest that while we may wish to hold firm to traditional standard English, it may no longer be possible to do so. Regardless, a respectful teacher would place her personal feelings "on the back burner" and teach awareness of each group's uniqueness.

16. Match the theorists with the elements of their explanations. (Place the letter after the number.)
(Rigorous) (Skill 3.1)

1. _____ Chomsky
2. _____ Piaget
3. _____ Vygotsky
4. _____ Collier

A. Children are active learners who construct their worlds.
B. Social communication promotes language and cognition.
C. Nature is more important than nurture.
D. Language is a reflection of thought.

Answers: A-3, B-4, C-2, D-1.

17. **The difference between learning a language and acquiring it is best illustrated by the example of:**
(Rigorous) (Skill *3.2)*

   A. Studying the grammar of a language instead of learning it through reading, TV, etc.
   B. Children using language in play compared to an adult watching a movie.
   C. A child sounding out words and an adult helping the child with pronunciation.
   D. An immigrant trying to learn the language while at work compared to a child learning the language at school.

   Answer: A. Studying the grammar of a language instead of learning it through reading, TV, etc.

   This question refers to Krashen's Acquisition-Learning Hypothesis, part of his theory of second language acquisition which states that children "acquire" a second language using the same process they used to learn their first language, while adults who have already learned one language will often have to "learn" the language through coursework, studying and memorizing. Option A is correct.

18. **Which of the following periods of speech is being developed by the following activity?**
(Rigorous) (Skill 3.2)

   Activity: The teacher tapes a short story of approximately 200-300 words to the wall at some distance from the students. She then divides the group into pairs. One student goes to the story and reads it. The first student (the runner) returns to his or her partner and dictates the story. Since it is unlikely that an ELL will remember the whole story exactly, the runner must make several trips.

   A. Private speech.
   B. Lexical chunks.
   C. Experimental or simplified speech.
   D. Formulaic speech.

   Answer: B. Lexical chunks.

   Private speech (A) occurs when the learner knows about 1000 words and speaks in one-or two-word phrases. This is an early production stage. Options B and C are more advanced levels of speaking. However, despite improved ability in speaking and fluency, it is unlikely that the ELL will remember sentence structure or the grammar of the text to be dictated. Thus, the activity illustrated is aimed at developing the ability of the ELL to remember lexical chunks in order to dictate them to his partner. Option B is the correct choice.

19. **Which of the following does NOT illustrate the role of L1 on L2 learning? (Rigorous) (Skill 3.3)**

    A. High school students may do well orally, but be unable to understand written materials.
    B. A gifted 5-year-old student is approximately halfway through his L1 language development.
    C. An ELL who has not matured in his or her L1 has not acquired the subtleties of phonological distinctions.
    D. Students who do not reach a certain level of knowledge in L1, including literacy, will have less difficulty acquiring a new language if it is introduced with L1.

    Answer: D. Students who do not reach a certain level of knowledge in L1, including literacy, will have less difficulty acquiring a new language if it is introduced with L1.

    ELLs need time to learn their native or heritage language just as any other speaker learning their native language. When language studies in their L1 are interrupted (possibly by coming to the U.S. at an early age), ELLs are at a disadvantage in acquiring the knowledge necessary to function in the rigorous U.S. school system, and learn a new language at the same time. Therefore, Option D is the correct one.

20. **An English Language Learner who has been living in the United States for many years is making little progress in her ESOL class. Her family and friends live in the same neighborhood as many of her relatives from her native land. Which one of the following conditions would probably have the most positive effect on the student's English language development? (Rigorous) (Skill 3.4)**

    A. Reducing the time spent listening to and viewing media in the native language.
    B. Decreasing the use of the native language in the home.
    C. Adopting external elements of the U. S. culture such as music and clothing.
    D. Increasing social contact with members of the U. S. culture.

    Answer: D. Increasing social contact with members of the U. S. culture.

    The amount of comprehensible input and output (linguistic variables) and the extent of connections with the new culture (sociocultural variables) affect language learning considerably. By developing new relationships with members of the U.S. culture, ELLs are able to hear and use their new language in meaningful contexts in their daily lives, both of which are key elements in the development of L2.

21. Communication involves specific skills such as:
(Average) (Skill 3.5)

    A. Turn-taking.
    B. Silent period.
    C. Lexical chunks.
    D. Repetition.

Answer: A. Turn-taking.

The silent period refers to a pre-production period observed before the ELL begins communicating. Lexical chunks are blocks of language used in everyday speech and writing. Repetition is used as a clarification technique or a stalling technique before the ELL is ready to proceed. All are part of the language acquisition process. There are many skills involved in communication, but the only one listed is turn-taking.

22. Angela needs help in English. Her teacher suggested several things Angela can do to improve her learning strategies. One of the following is NOT a socioaffective learning strategy.
(Easy) (Skill 3.6)

    A. Read a funny book.
    B. Work cooperatively with her classmates.
    C. Ask the teacher to speak more slowly.
    D. Skim for information.

Answer: D. Skim for information.

Options A, B and C are all socioaffective learning strategies. Answer D is a cognitive strategy and the correct choice.

23. An ESOL teacher who encourages her students to keep track of their progress in English Language Learning is stimulating which learning strategy?
(Rigorous) (Skill 3.6)

    A. Metacognitive.
    B. Affective.
    C. Cognitive.
    D. Social

Answer: A. Metacognitive.

This ESOL teacher is instructing her ELLs in strategies that make them aware of their individual learning. By being aware of their learning strategies, ELLs can compare their previous learning with their actual learning and measure their progress (or lack of).

24. Research shows that error correction in ELLs is a delicate business. Which of the following contributes to learning? Correction of:
(Rigorous) (Skill 3.7)

    A. Semantic errors.
    B. Grammatical errors.
    C. Pronunciation.
    D. All written work errors.

Answer: A. Semantic errors.

The correction of semantic errors leads to increased vocabulary and L2 learning. All other options listed have been proven to be ineffective.

25. Which of the following approaches is based on using cognitive processes to solve problems?
(Rigorous) (Skill 4.1)

A. Total Physical Response.
B. Learning Experience Approach.
C. CALLA.
D. Gap activities.

Answer: D. Gap activities.

Pradhu is the leading proponent of using gap activities to solve cognitive problems in the language learning process. His research demonstrates that language, both communicative and linguistic competence, is acquired by interacting with meaning. Prabhu divides gap activities into information-gap tasks, reasoning-gap tasks, and opinion-gap tasks.

26. Which of the following is NOT a manifestation of affective variables?
(Average) (Skill 4.2)

A. Anxiety.
B. Self-esteem.
C. Cognition.
D. Attitude.

Answer: C. Cognition.

A, B, and D are all affective variables. Only C is a cognitive one.

27. Which of the following best describes "facilitative" anxiety?
(Average) (Skill 4.2)

A. Juan always seems anxious and usually fails his tests.
B. Juanita hesitates to speak in front of her classmates.
C. Pedro looks worried all the time, but he usually does well on his tests.
D. Maria looks perplexed and seems lost in class. She cries a lot.

Answer: C. Pedro looks worried all the time, but he usually does well on his tests.

A, B, C and D are all examples of how anxiety affects students. A, B, and D are cases where the anxiety negatively affects school work. Option D is the best choice because Pedro uses his anxiety in a positive (facilitative) way to "stay on task" and succeed in his academic work.

28. Which of the following factors is NOT a social factor affecting an ELL's language learning capabilities?
(Average) (Skill 4.3)

A. Gender.
B. Social class.
C. Age.
D. Level of English.

Answer: D. Level of English.

A, B, and C are social factors which affect an ELL's language learning. His or her level of English does not.

29. Which of the following indicates the learning style of an ELL who is interested in mathematics, can see planes in algebra, and can understand what an author means but does not specifically express?
(Rigorous) (Skill 4.4)

A. Concrete.
B. Analytic.
C. Communicative.
D. Authority-oriented.

Answer: B. Analytic.

According to Willing (1988,) an analytic learning style is found in a person who is object-oriented, with a capacity for making connections and inferences. All of these variables coincide with a person who is good at understanding the concrete and abstract features of mathematics.

30. **Which of the following statements is most accurate, according to the latest research on learner variables?**
(Rigorous) (Skill 4.4)

   A. Age determines when an ELL learns specific grammar points.
   B. The best language learners are young children.
   C. The most efficient language learners are teens.
   D. Teens learn to pronounce the language more accurately than adults or children.

   Answer: C. The most efficient language learners are teens.

   Contrary to what many people believe, children are not the best language learners. Their pronunciation and willingness to experiment with language makes them good at pronunciation, but they do not have the life experience that teens and adults have. Teens and older learners are, therefore, more efficient at learning a new language than children because of their previous experience with how language works. Teens also surpass both older learners and children in grammar acquisition.

31. **Inter-language is best described as:**
(Easy) (Skill 4.5)

   A. A language characterized by overgeneralization.
   B. Bilingualism.
   C. A language learning strategy.
   D. A strategy characterized by poor grammar.

   Answer: C. A language learning strategy.

   Inter-language occurs when the second language learner lacks proficiency in L2 and tries to compensate for his or her lack of fluency in the new language. Three components are overgeneralization, simplification, and L1 interference or language transfer. Answer A is only one component of inter-language, making option C the correct answer.

32. Upon arrival in a new country, immigrants frequently show signs of _____ in order to get a job.
(Easy) (Skill 5.1)

A. Assimilation.
B. Acculturation.
C. Transculturation.
D. Accommodation.

Answer: D. Accommodation.

While new immigrants acquire the skills they need to succeed in their new culture, they may accommodate their cultural heritage to the new one. Later, as they are more fully integrated into the host society, they may begin to feel less intimidated and demonstrate their heritage culture more openly.

33. Which of the following terms is the correct one for the situation below?
(Rigorous) (Skill 5.1)

Situation: Ursula has lived in the U.S. for nearly five years. She rarely talks about her homeland and tries to imitate her classmates' speech and behavior. She is striving to be accepted by the culture surrounding her.

A. Acculturation.
B. Assimilation.
C. Accommodation.
D. Transculturation.

Answer: B. Assimilation.

Ursula is making an effort to be like those around her. Her willingness to imitate her classmates' speech and behavior shows her desire to be accepted by her peers. Given her willingness to act like her classmates, Ursula seems to be highly motivated to "fit in" or assimilate.

34. Culture and cultural differences:
(Average) (Skill 5.2)

A. Must be addressed by the teacher in the ELL classroom by pointing out cultural similarities and differences.
B. Should be the starting point for learning about how culture affects ELLs' attitudes5 towards education.
C. Positively affects how well ELLs perform in the language classroom.
D. May have strong emotional influence on the ELL learner.

Answer: D. May have strong emotional influence on the ELL learner.

Culture and cultural differences may be addressed by the skillful ESOL teacher, but frequently teachers are unaware of all the cultures and cultural differences they are dealing with. It may be possible to determine how his or her culture affects the ELL's attitude towards education; however, it may be something the young child cannot express or the adult hides for various reasons. Culture and cultural differences do not always play a positive role in the learning process. Culture and cultural differences may have a strong emotional influence on the ELL learner, whether it be negative or positive. Thus, D is our best option.

35. Which of the following statements about culture and its manifestations is most likely to cause learning difficulties in the ELL?
(Average) (Skill 5.2)

A. Culture is synonymous with learning a language.
B. ELLs may not understand culture and its differences.
C. Teachers may offend students when they ignore cultural differences.
D. ELLs often believe their culture is superior to the one they are learning.

Answer: C. Teachers may offend students when they ignore cultural differences.

Teaching ELLs is a rewarding and challenging profession. Often, however, because of their own lack of understanding of cultural manifestations, teachers unwittingly cause barriers to language learning by offending their students without knowing that they have. Therefore, all teachers who are involved in the education of ELLs need to learn as much as they can about the foreign culture, if for no other reason than to demonstrate respect for their students' cultures.

36. **Which of the following cultural elements most likely explains the situation below?**
(Easy) (Skill 5.3)

Situation: Amelia is conscientious in her studies, but she can't seem to finish on time, and gets angry when the teacher tells her to hand in her paper.

A. Family structure.
B. Roles and interpersonal relationships.
C. Discipline.
D. Time.

Answer: D. Time.

In many cultures, time and its distinct manifestations (such as 'being on time) is of little importance. Oftentimes, these students are allowed as much time as they need to finish a quiz or assignment. Teaching time limitations on testing and class work may be a long, difficult process for ELLs from cultures where time is given so little consideration.

37. **Pierre arrived in the U. S. in 2005. He has been living with his uncle and aunt, who are well assimilated into the U.S. culture. Pierre misses his parents and brothers. He finds his high school studies fairly easy and his classmates lazy. He is worried about his goal of becoming a professional soccer player and doesn't understand why he can't have wine with his meals when he eats out with his aunt and uncle. In which stage of assimilation is Pierre?**
(Average) (Skill 5.4)

A. Honeymoon stage.
B. Hostility stage.
C. Humor stage.
D. Home stage.

Answer: B. Hostility stage.

While Pierre is probably adapting, he still finds his culture superior ("His classmates are lazy" and "why he can't have wine with his meal') and the new culture deficient ("worried about his goal of becoming a professional soccer player").

38. **ESOL instruction frequently requires the teacher to change her instruction methods. One of the most difficult may be the:**
   (Rigorous) (Skill 5.5)

   A. Wait time.
   B. Establishment of group work.
   C. Show and tell based on different cultures.
   D. Extensive reading time.

   Answer: A. Wait time.

   Answer B, C, and D can all be discounted since they are standard practice for language arts teachers. Answer A, the amount of time a teacher waits for an answer from her students, can be very difficult to change. Teachers may be somewhat impatient ("Let's get on with it"), lack understanding ("If they knew the answer, they would respond"), and unaware of differences between the U.S. and other cultures. Answer A is the correct response.

39. **Which activity could be used to explore the cultural heritage of many diverse countries?**
   (Average) (Skill 5.1)

   A. Singing "Hava Nagila".
   B. Composing original parodies (e.g., 'On Top of Spaghetti').
   C. Comparing proverbs from different countries.
   D. Writing Haiku poems.

   Answer: C. Comparing proverbs from different countries.

   Answers A, B, and C are country specific. Option C provides the opportunity to comparing proverbs from different countries. By demonstrating to ELLs and their classmates that many countries share similar sayings or proverbs on universal topics, we are sponsoring the idea of cultural unity.

40. **Which of the following best describes linguistic imperialism? The loss of native or heritage languages:**
(Rigorous) (Skill 6.1)

   A. Due to the influence of other, dominant languages.
   B. Because of the Internet.
   C. Because of the globalization of goods and trade.
   D. Due to the limited resources of the native or heritage culture.

Answer: A. Due to the influence of other, dominant languages.

While there is little agreement about the number of languages in the world (estimates vary between 4000 and 5000), linguists do agree that languages are being lost in the face of Western exploration. British colonialism, the Internet and globalization are among the many factors in the spread of English around the world. This has caused a dominance of English in all areas of modern cultures. The dominance of English has caused the loss of national languages and resentment in some of these cultures. Thus, minority languages face a two-pronged attack: modern cultures imposing upon weaker, more primitive cultures and their languages as well as the spread of English to facilitate communication in all areas of modern life such as business, transportation, travel, and education.

41. **Which of the following relationships would probably cause the least conflict for an immigrant in the U. S.?**
(Average) (Skill 6.2)

   A. School.
   B. Religious beliefs.
   C. Workplace relationships.
   D. Desire for better status for future.

Answer: D. Desire for better status for future.
Schools, religious beliefs and workplace relationships all have their own power structures, roles, and statuses that can challenge the ingrained cultural beliefs of immigrants. Because of the desire to obtain a better status in the future, many immigrants are willing to make considerable sacrifice in order to obtain a safer, more secure, or higher status life in the future for themselves and their families.

42. **Which of the following is NOT a method for discovering a person's height in English speaking cultures?**
(Easy) (Skill 6.4)

A. Measuring another's height by comparing shoulder heights.
B. Measuring two people back-to-back.
C. Stating a person is almost as tall as someone else.
D. Holding the hand out with the thumb pointing upward.

Answer: D. Holding the hand out with the thumb pointing upward.

In some Latin American countries, animals are measured by holding the hand out, palm down. To discuss people, the hand is held vertically with the thumb pointing towards the ceiling or sky.

43. **Which of the following strategies provides the ELL with the opportunity to celebrate his/her native culture and the US culture at the same time?**
(Rigorous) (Skill 6.4)

A. ELL-created role plays highlighting common cultural misunderstandings.
B. A telephone conversation between a foreign customer and a U.S. company read from a textbook.
C. A learning diary about the ELL's difficulties in English.
D. Teacher assigned research on different cultures.

Answer: A. ELL-created role plays highlighting common cultural misunderstandings.

The telephone conversation read from a textbook is not considered to be authentic language because it does not permit the participants to interact with each other in a natural setting. The learning diary provides excellent one-on-one contact between the teacher and the student. Research on different cultures is an excellent learning device for students who can read. Nevertheless, Option A would provide the ELLs with the opportunity to interact with their peers, poke fun at or explain their culture to a U.S. audience, and use their creative powers in writing and acting. Option A is the best choice.

44. Which of the following statements are examples of stereotyping? (Rigorous) (Skill 7.3)

A. All U.S. citizens are educated.
B. All Latinos can dance.
C. All Europeans speak several languages.
D. All of the above

Answer: D. All of the above.

All three statements are examples of stereotyping.

45. The decision by which the US Supreme Court essentially mandated bilingual instruction was: (Easy) (Skill 7.1)

A. The Civil Rights Act.
B. Lau v. Nichols.
C. Castaneda v. Pickard.
D. No Child Left Behind.

Answer: B. Lau v Nichols.

In this decision, the U.S. Supreme Court found that Chinese ELLs were denied an equal education because their instruction was in a language they could not understand. The ruling was that "identical" education is not necessarily "equal" education and schools must take steps to overcome educational barriers to LEPs.

46. The No Child Left Behind Act established that:
(Rigorous) (Skill 7.1)

A. Title I funds are available only if the schools participate in National Assessment of Education Progress.
B. Bilingual programs must be effective within three specific criteria.
C. High performance children cannot be used to average out low-performing ELLs.
D. Schools must form and convene assessment committees.

Answer: C. High performance children cannot be used to average out low-performing ELLs.

Selection A refers to the establishment of voluntary school participation in NAEP after the National Committee on Excellence in Education produced their report, ***A Nation at Risk*** (1983). Selection B refers to the decision rendered in Castaneda v Pickard (1981). One requirement resulting from Lau v Nichols (1974) was that schools must form and convene assessment committees. The NCLB act specifically states that disaggregated data must be used in evaluating school performance.

47. In contrast to many state positions, the federal government advocates _____ for ELLs:
(Average) (Skill 7.1)

A. Higher funding for inner-city schools.
B. Equal opportunities and protection.
C. Restructuring of school districts.
D. A technologically prepared workforce.

Answer: B. Equal opportunities and protection.

48. In schools with large immigrant populations of diverse origin, the most commonly used model is:
(Average) (Skill 7.2)

A. Submersion.
B. Pull-out ESL.
C. SDAIE.
D. Transition.

Answer: B. Pull-out ESL.

SDAIE or Specially Designed Academic Programs in English is the structured immersion model most commonly used in California. The submersion model does not provide the necessary support that ELLs need and is in disfavor. Transition models provided approximately three years of BICs but frequently leave the LEP with almost no support while learning CALPs. Today, the most commonly used model is B: Pull-out ESL.

49. CALLA is an example of which of the following models used to instruct ELLs?
(Average) (Skill 7.2)

A. Structured English immersion.
B. Communication-based ESL.
C. Submersion with primary language support.
D. Content-based ESL.

Answer: D. Content-based ESL.

Content-based ESL is designed to teach content to ELLs and prepare them for grade-level content materials in English. The emphasis is on language, but using content materials, vocabulary, and basic concepts. CALLA is an example of this education model.

50. **Which of the following is one of the goals of the International Baccalaureate Program?**
    (Rigorous) (Skill 7.3)

    A. Promote the teaching of English abroad.
    B. Encourage foreign students to learn English well.
    C. Permit foreign students to study English as native speakers do.
    D. Standardize content areas in schools of diverse countries.

    Answer: D. Standardize content areas in schools of diverse countries.

    One of the goals of the International Baccalaureate Program is to provide a standardized high school program suitable for the growing mobile population of young people of diverse countries between the ages of 16 and 19. The program is especially helpful to those students who plan to enter the university in a foreign country (e.g. Great Britain) and to those whose parents are engaged in diplomacy, world business, or the military.

51. **Which of the following is a key element in professional development? (Average) (Skill 7.4)**

    A. Consulting a mentor.
    B. Creating a portfolio.
    C. Joining professional support groups, (e.g., TESOL).
    D. Planning and writing down goals.

    Answer: D. Planning and writing down goals.

    While all the answers are helpful in achieving professional development, research has proven that the single most important factor is planning and writing down goals.

52. Which of the following is NOT the role of the ESOL resource person? (Average) (Skill 7.5)

A. Encouraging a text-rich environment.
B. Maintaining an ample supply of realia.
C. Conducting workshops on discourse analysis.
D. Reporting a suspected case of child abuse.

Answer: D. Reporting a suspected case of child abuse.

The ESOL professional is a resource person for the entire school community of educators who may be dubious when confronted with ELLs in their classroom. However, ALL teachers have the moral and legal responsibility to report suspected cases of child abuse to their superiors.

53. Homeroom teacher A enjoys teaching literature while homeroom teacher B enjoys teaching mathematics. Which of the following teaching models might best accommodate their preferences? (Rigorous) (Skill 7.6)

A. One teach, one assist.
B. Parallel teaching.
C. Team teaching.
D. One teach, one observe.

Answer: C. Team teaching.

No one teaching model has been proven more effective than another. In this case, the teachers may be more comfortable with team teaching if there are strong preferences about what they like to teach.

54. **A newly immigrated family has expressed the desire to mingle with native-speaking Americans in order to polish their English speaking skills. Which one of the following actions would probably be the most appropriate and effective in addressing the mother's and father's needs to mingle with native-speaking Americans?**
(Easy) (Skill 8.1)

A. Suggest a private class in their home.
B. Provide literature about the programs offered at the local mall for diet and exercise.
C. Mention the YMCA/YWCA and their services.
D. Recommend the public library and its adult programs.

Answer: D. Recommend the public library and its adult programs.

Suggesting programs about diet and exercise or sports would not be the best choices, unless the ESOL teacher is asked specifically about them. The public library would probably be the best choice for introducing adults to a world wider than the native-speaking community. Libraries have a variety of services that would serve many needs. Depending on the local facilities, libraries offer adult education programs, book clubs for scholars, children's sections for harried mothers, and computer classes.

55. An English Language Learner who is a recent immigrant to the United States has been given a placement test and placed in the intermediate ESOL level. She is in high school and her other test results suggest an advanced placement in biology, which she claims to really like. The science teacher is reluctant to accept her in his class because of her English level. He is worried that she will be unable to understand the course materials. Which of the following approaches would be the most effective for the ESOL teacher to use to help the student?
(Average) (Skill 8.2)

A. Offering to work closely with the biology teacher to provide the ELL with the English language support she needs to take the advanced course.
B. Suggesting the student take a lower level science course until her language skills test at the advanced level.
C. Asking the biology teacher to provide advanced-level biology materials that the ESOL teacher could include in the ELL's language instruction.
D. Recommending that the student focus on developing her English language skills before attempting advanced content coursework.

Answer: A. Offering to work closely with the biology teacher to provide the ELL with the English language support she needs to take the advanced course.

A key charge of the ESOL teacher is to work closely with other teachers to provide the best and most challenging educational opportunities possible for ELLs. To do so, the ESOL teacher must work closely with other teachers helping them understand the academic, social, and emotional challenges faced by ELLs. Together they can plan strategies for helping the ELLs overcome these difficulties.

56. The teacher of an eighth-grade class in public school ABC has six Asian, and three Latino ELLs with very low English skills. Each student is from a different country. Which of the following educational model would probably serve the ELLs best?
(Average) (Skill 8.2)

A. Pull-out model
B. Resource center/lab
C. Cluster center
D. Scheduled class period only

Answer: B. Resource center/lab.

Because of the diversity of the student population, a resource center and/or language lab would probably be the best option for serving the ELLs. In the resource center or language lab, materials specific to each student's needs could be located and at the same time allow the ESOL teacher to work with the whole group.

57. Which of the following is a software translating program that could be helpful to ELLs?
(Rigorous) (Skill 8.3)

A. SimCity.
B. Fast ForWord.
C. Babel Fish.
D. Content Mania.

Answer: C. Babel Fish.

Babel Fish is a translation program that supports learning, especially for those groups of ELLs where there is no native language resource person, and who are having difficulty in grasping concepts or understanding vocabulary

58. Which one point is the aim of the 2009 version of the Dream Act? (Rigorous) (Skill 8.4)

A. Promote military service or college education of older illegal immigrants.
B. Permit children who immigrated to the U.S. at an early age to acquire legal status independently of their parents.
C. Encourage good moral character from undocumented immigrants.
D. Advocate education for legal aliens.

Answer: B. Permit children who immigrated to the U.S. at an early age to acquire legal status independently of their parents.

The Dream Act has had its ups and downs, but it promises to legalize children who, through no fault of their own, are being raised in a "foreign" country, though it may be the only home they have known. The act would apply only to minors who are of good moral character and under certain other conditions.

59. The school is planning a "Grandparents Day.'" Which of the following activities could be best used to promote the ESOL program? (Easy) (Skill 8.5)

A. A bake sale.
B. Sports activities, (e.g., yoga, soccer, etc.)
C. Skits by children.
D. Simple board games incorporating ESOL techniques in the game.

Answer: D. Simple board games incorporating ESOL techniques in the game.

Options A, B, and C are all traditional activities for interesting families in their children's school. Option D would offer the grandparents the opportunity to read and ask questions about the ESOL program of their grandchildren. Remember, TESOL (in all its distinct forms: ESL, EFL, EAP, ESOL, in addition to TESOL) has changed tremendously since the days of grammar/translation, which may be the only form of language learning the grandparents are familiar with.

60. **Based on the last two years' test scores, school XYZ has ranked near the bottom in the district. Which of the following strategies would be most appropriate for involving the community in turning the school around? (Easy) (Skill 8.6)**

   A. A series of lectures and newsletters in the native language of the students.
   B. Increased security.
   C. Involving the older members of the community in mentoring or tutoring programs.
   D. Inviting high profile sports figures to speak on the value of education.

   Answer: C. Involving the older members of the community in mentoring or tutoring programs.

   Schools are where community members transmit much of their culture. Schools are where community members send their children in the quest for a more successful future. In many societies, the older members of the society are highly respected for their wisdom. Grandparents frequently are the caregivers for young children whose parents must work. Yet, many older people feel alienated by "being put out to pasture" while they believe they still have much to offer. By mentoring or tutoring young children, grandparents provide the schools a valuable free resource.

61. **An ELL in middle school has been in the United States for two years but has recently been transferred to a new school. He seems to do well in most classes, but has difficulties in math. What would be the most appropriate strategy to help him learn the content-related material? (Rigorous) (Skill 9.1)**

   A. Provide intensive vocabulary instruction on the relevant material.
   B. Activate background knowledge.
   C. Explain the concepts in his native language.
   D. Arrange for a pull-out period with other ELLs.

   Answer: A. Provide intensive vocabulary instruction on the relevant material.

   Since the ELL has already been in school in the U.S. for two years and is doing well in most classes, he may be struggling with the specific vocabulary and language of mathematics.   Intensive vocabulary instruction in the content area may help alleviate his problems.

62. Advanced TPR might include:
(Easy) (Skill 9.2)

A. Rapid fire commands.
B. More advanced vocabulary.
C. Funny commands.
D. All of the above.

Answer: D. All of the above.

Total Physical Response can be done slowly as a beginning activity for ELLs. As they begin to understand more oral English and the game, TPR can be "spiced up" by any or all of the suggestions.

63. Which of the following best describes the goal of CALLA?
(Easy) (Skill 9.2)

A. Active learning in the regular classroom.
B. Full participation in ESOL classes.
C. Math studies for advanced ELLs.
D. Transition from ESOL language programs to regular classroom programs.

Answer: D. Transition from ESOL language programs to regular classroom programs.

The Cognitive Academic Language Learning Approach (CALLA) is a program designed to facilitate the learning of English using content area materials. However, it is to a transitional program whose goal is to "mainstream" the ELL as soon as possible.

64. **Which of the following instructional approaches emphasizes LEPs working on content?**
(Average) (Skill 9.2)

A. TPR.
B. The Natural Approach.
C. CALLA.
D. The Communicative Approach.

Answer: C. CALLA.

CALLA is the brain-child of Chamot and O'Malley. Their work is based on the principle that the child learns far more language in content classes than in ESOL pull-out classes. CALLA (Cognitive Academic Language Learning Approach) integrates language development, content area instruction and explicit instruction in learning strategies.

65. **A parent filled out the home language survey as indicated below:**

Is a language other than English used in the home? Yes.
Does the student have a first language other than English? Yes.
Does the student most frequently speak a language other than English? No.

What is the school's next step?
(Rigorous) (Skill 9.3)

A. Placing the student at grade level with no assessment.
B. Postponing admission until testing is completed.
C. Assigning the student to an ESOL program while beginning testing.
D. Placing the student in the grade-level ESOL program.

Answer: C. Assigning to an ESOL program while beginning testing.

Answers A (placing the student at grade-level with no assessment) and D (placing in the grade-level ESOL program) do an injustice to the ELL, as the student has been given no chance to demonstrate his or her capabilities. Answer B is equally inappropriate as the child has the right to schooling. Answer C is the appropriate selection since the ELL's rights to an education are being protected while the most appropriate environment is being determined.

66. **Which of the following options is best for the ESOL teacher to use to activate background knowledge?**
(Average) (Skill 9.3)

A. Demonstrating, using realia.
B. Asking questions about the topic using a picture to illustrate the topic.
C. Reading the text with the ELL and explaining as you go.
D. Allowing the ELL to watch a video on the school intranet.

Answer: A. Demonstrating, using realia.

All of the activities will activate background knowledge if done well with appropriate materials. Even so, using authentic materials while seeing and touching real objects as they are being discussed or used in demonstrations is the best option for activating background knowledge.

67. **The 5th grade content area teacher has decided to use stories in her classroom for all students. What would be the best strategy to use so that the ELLs also participate?**
(Rigorous) (Skill 9.4)

A. Discuss favorite stories with the class.
B. Bring in picture books of children's stories.
C. Have children draw their own stories.
D. Group the students together and have them retell their favorite movies.

Answer: D. Group the students together and have them retell their favorite movies.

When students are grouped, it lessens the pressure of performing for the entire class. By discussing a favorite movie, the students are given the chance to use language as they would in a natural context. Even underprivileged ELLs have access to a TV and/or movies that they can relate to others using the language they know to talk about something they enjoyed. .

68. **Which of the following is the best option for introducing new vocabulary to pre-literate ELLs?**
    (Easy) (Skill 9.4)

    A. Wall charts.
    B. Word ladders.
    C. Stories.
    D. Spelling lists.

    Answer: C. Stories.

    Wall charts and word ladders are excellent scaffolding devices for helping ELLs remember the words they are studying. Spelling lists help them remember specific words and how to spell them. Option C is the best option for introducing new words. Here the ELLs get the opportunity to see the words used in context and later learn the ones they don't already know.

69. **Which of the following best illustrates how ESOL teachers can help all their ELLs feel the classroom is a safe, welcoming environment?**
    (Rigorous) (Skill 9.5)

    A. Learning corners are set up around the room for free exploration.
    B. The ESOL area is a rich environment with materials about the ELL's homeland.
    C. A companion is assigned to each ELL to help them learn where things are and what to do in social situations.
    D. The ESOL instructor corrects the ELL's oral language and keeps track of the errors they commit.

    Answer: C. A companion is assigned to each ELL to help them learn where things are and what to do in social situations.

    Options A and B address helping the ELL with academics. Option D is a poor practice since the ESOL instructor should correct written errors and permit oral fluency as much as possible in order to overcome the feelings of anxiety and distress that come from being in stressful, new situations. Thus, the best Option is C.

70. **Which is the best option to improve ELLs English language skills overall? (Rigorous) (Skill 9.6)**

    A. Reports on something familiar to them such as their home country or a friend.
    B. Choral recitation of dialogs.
    C. Practice in writing dictated passages.
    D. Drills using TPR.

    Answer: A. Reports on something familiar to them such as their home country or a friend.

    Options B, C, and D have their place in the ESOL classroom. Option A addresses the overall performance of ELL's oral speech. Given the opportunity to organize their thoughts about something familiar to them, they may be willing to share with the class and thereby use the language skills they have in a non-threatening way.

71. **An ESOL teacher wants to have her ELLs work in small groups. Which of the following techniques/resources would provide the best support to the students? (Rigorous) (Skill 9.7)**

    A. Internet research facilities.
    B. Library access.
    C. Bilingual dictionaries.
    D. Interactive scaffolding.

    Answer: D. Interactive scaffolding.

    Options A, B, and C are good resources for all students, including ELLs. Since many ELLs suffer from anxieties and worry about their language abilities, they probably receive the most benefit from interactive scaffolding where they can ask the ESOL teacher how to say something, where to find information, and whether something is correct.

72. In order for the class to complete a unit on mammals, the content area teacher wanted the class to write. Which activity would be the most challenging way to test learning while incorporating other language skills in the activity?
(Rigorous) (Skill 9.8)

A.   A summary of a written text in a graphic form.
B. A drawing with a short paragraph explaining the drawing.
C. A letter to the editor of the daily paper.
D. A dialogue between two animals.

Answer: A. A summary of a written text in a graphic form.

All of the options are ways of analyzing the student's learning. Option A incorporates the student's higher reasoning abilities by calling for information transfer from a written text to a graphic form. As the learners may have to meet criteria of completeness and correctness, it is a good way to evaluate them.

73. Which of the following would be the best option for an authentic response to the topic of endangered species?
(Rigorous) (Skill 9.8)

A. Draw your favorite endangered animal and explain why it is your favorite.
B. Write a dialogue between two people discussing the problems associated with endangered animals.
C. Write a letter to the magazine of the Sierra Club.
D. Write a journal entry expressing your personal feelings.

Answer: C. Write a letter to the magazine of the Sierra Club.

Authenticity is an important component of tasks in the classroom. Requesting that students write a letter to the Sierra Club provides an opportunity to engage in a "real-life" task that many adults use to express their opinions on subjects of importance to them.

74. **Which one of the following features of texts is NOT user-friendly for beginning readers?**
   (Rigorous) (Skill 10.1)

   Texts which:

   A. Summarize key points.
   B. Have highlighted vocabulary.
   C. Use advanced vocabulary.
   D. Contain new vocabulary.

   Answer: C. Use advanced vocabulary.

   Struggling readers (including ELLs) need texts which are user-friendly.
   Options A, B, and D contain elements which make the text easier for readers.
   Option C does not.

75. **When using concept maps, the students must learn to _____ the different elements of the topic.**
   (Average) (Skill 10.1)

   A. Rank.
   B. Organize.
   C. Evaluate.
   D. Associate.

   Answer: A. Rank

   Concept maps differ from webbing by requiring that relationships between words and phrases be ranked in order of importance from the most general to the most specific.

76. **When an ESOL teacher is helping an ELL to understand material that is difficult for them, which of the following theorist's principals is the teacher implementing?**
(Rigorous) (Skill 10.2)

A. Cummins.
B. Vygotsky.
C. Tompkins.
D. Krashen.

Answer: D. Krashen.

Krashen proposed that ELLs need to be instructed at a level slightly above their understanding (e.g., i + 1). By helping ELLs understand material that is difficult for them, the ESOL teacher is instructing at this level.

77. **Which of the following operations is the ESOL teacher using when she teaches the concept of "mother/madre/mere"?**
(Rigorous) (Skill 10.3)

A. Cognates.
B. Nominalization.
C. Vocabulary.
D. Idioms.

Answer: A. Cognates.

For the ESOL instructor who knows the comparable words in the language of her students, instruction in cognates is an excellent way to increase vocabulary. However, there are false cognates (the Spanish word '"libreria" means "bookstore", not "library") of which one must beware.

78. **When teaching ELLs the same content as mainstream students, but using different types of resources, the ESOL teacher is helping the ELLs in which of the following ways?**
    (Rigorous) (Skill 10.3)

    A. By creating different learning goals.
    B. By appealing to the different senses.
    C. By recognizing and using different intelligences.
    D. By employing different learning styles.

    Answer: C. By recognizing and using different intelligences.

    Gardner's work on multiple intelligences affirms that learners have different learning styles and ways of perceiving information. Therefore, teachers should provide a wide variety of materials that appeal to the different senses and intelligences. In doing so, they provide access to what the student may know, but not recognize in a different format.

79. **Which is NOT a category of the K-W-L chart?**
    (Easy) (Skill 10.4)

    A. List what you want to know.
    B. List what you learned.
    C. List what you must learn.
    D. List what you know.

    Answer: C. List what you must learn.

80. **When considering using technology in the classroom, which of the following criteria is most important for the ESOL teacher keep in mind? (Rigorous) (Skill 10.5)**

    A. Is the technology (e.g. the Internet) the most efficient method of teaching the material?
    B. Is the project designed with the learner in mind?
    C. Will you be able to communicate by Internet with each student personally at least once a month?
    D. Will this project contribute to the ELLs learning portfolio?

Answer: A. Is the technology (e.g., the Internet) the most efficient method of teaching the material?

The Internet is a tool and as educators, the first question we must ask ourselves is "Is this the best tool for the purpose I have in mind? ". If not, other options must be explored.

81. **Which of the following is NOT an acceptable alternative assessment strategy for ELLs? (Average) (Skill 11.1)**

    A. Portfolios.
    B. Observation.
    C. Self-assessment.
    D. Essay writing.

Answer: D. Essay writing.

A and B provide alternative assessment over a period of time. C is a form of self-analysis which may help the learner recognize some of his or her weakness as well as strengths. Only option D is inappropriate for the ELL as an alternative method of assessment.

82. Which of the following is the most appropriate method for aligning instruction with assessment?
(Average) (Skill 11.2)

A. The ESOL instructor teaches the students from their "needs" level.
B. The content area instructor fully informs the ESOL instructor of the curriculum requirements.
C. The content area teacher provides vocabulary lists to the ESOL instructor.
D. The ESOL teacher instructs the ELLs in content area materials based on their needs.

Answer: B. The content area instructor fully informs the ESOL instructor of the curriculum requirements.

High-stakes testing requires the coordinated involvement of all instructors in planning the curriculum goals for their students. In this case, the ESOL teacher needs to know exactly what is expected of the ELLs in order to plan and instruct them to meet their curriculum goals.

83. When testing for an ELL's level of English proficiency, which minor accommodation is appropriate?
(Rigorous) (Skill 11.3)

A. Allowing extra time if necessary.
B. Using the ELL's portfolio.
C. Recitation.
D. Providing translation of prompts as needed for understanding.

Answer: A. Allowing extra time if necessary.

Answers B and C suggest alternative testing methods. Answer D is inappropriate as the level of English proficiency is being tested. Answer A is the correct answer as ELLs may need more time to respond to questions until they become more familiar with the English language and U.S. testing situations.

84. **Which of the following characteristics may indicate an ELL who is gifted? (Average) (Skill 11.3)**

   A. Learns content well but has some language difficulties.
   B. Able to solve problems independently of the language (e.g., math problems)
   C. Good learner in heritage language.
   D. Good academic history from native land.

   Answer: D. Good academic history from native land.

   Answer D suggests that excellent academic work in their first language would be the prime indicator of a student with exceptional abilities, especially if those abilities are apparent in the L2 also.

85. **Which of the following tests is represented in the following example? Example: Students are required to listen to an announcement in a train station and fill in a chart. (Rigorous) (Skill 11.5)**

   A. Traditional tests.
   B. Criterion-referenced tests.
   C. Norm-referenced tests.
   D. Third generation tests.

   Answer: D. Third generation tests.

   Third generation tests are those in which a context is provided and integrative language is used. Thus, listening for information in an announcement made in a public place would be considered third-generation test.

86. **Before coming to the U.S., Sven, an 11th-grade student, took the TOEFL. This is a _____ test. (Easy) (Skill 11.6)**

   A. Language proficiency.
   B. Language achievement.
   C. Language placement.
   D. Diagnostic language.

   Answer: A. Language proficiency.

   Since the TOEFL tests a student's English language ability in reading comprehension, essay writing, syntax and lexis, it tests for language proficiency.

87. **Which of the following tests is an example of language achievement tests?**
(Average) (Skill 11.6)

A. A final exam.
B. Foreign Service Exam (FSI).
C. A placement test.
D. Test of Spoken English (TSE)

Answer: A. A final exam.

Options B and D are examples of proficiency tests. A placement test places students in the correct levels. Only final exams are achievement tests or tests which show what the student learned (or achieved) during a specific course of study.

88. **Which of the following statements is NOT correct?**
(Average) (Skill 11.7)

A. All ELLs are required to participate in all assessment programs.
B. All ELLs are allowed to defer assessment for one year.
C. WIDA tests ELLs' language skills in all four language domains.
D. Ending special services is usually based on a combination of performance criteria.

Answer: B. All ELLs are allowed to defer assessment for one year.

ELLs may be granted exemption status for one year, but it is not a given.

89. **Which method is most appropriate for dealing partially with cultural bias in tests?**
(Rigorous) (Skill 11.8)

A. Translate the tests previous to the actual exam.
B. Provide pictures and graphics during the test.
C. Administer practice tests with time limits.
D. Provide a study guide and give test orally.

Answer: C. Administer practice tests with time limits.

Answers A, B, and D are accommodations to the language deficiencies of ELLs, but do not address cultural bias. Answer C addresses cultural bias since many cultures do not time tests, and it is a norm in many U.S. testing environments.

90. **Which of the following test attributes is questioned when assessing an ELL's writing journal?**
    (Rigorous) (Skill 11.8)

    A. Practicality.
    B. Reliability.
    C. Concurrent validity.
    D. Predictive validity.

    Answer: A. Practicality.

    Assessing an ELL's writing journal may lead to problems of practicality. Since the subject matter is subjective, it may be difficult to grade. Also, as a premise of assessment is "test what you teach," the journal may not be representative of class work.

91. **What is the primary goal of the Georgia Alternate Assessment test?**
    (Average) (Skill 12.1)

    A. Provide ELLs in gifted programs access to more challenging curriculum.
    B. Administer a test to determine the placement of ELLs.
    C. Ensure all individuals access to the curriculum of the State of Georgia.
    D. Ensure all ELLs classified as individuals with disabilities an education.

    Answer: C. Ensure all individuals access to the curriculum of the State of Georgia.

    All students in the state of Georgia are provided with access to the state curriculum and granted the opportunity to work towards the achievement of state standards, including Individuals with disabilities under the Individuals with Disabilities Education Act (IDEA).

92. **Which of the following statements is NOT a valid reason for administering self-assessment tests?**
(Average) (Skill 12.2)

   A. It relieves the burden of assessment on the teacher.
   B. It provides useful information.
   C. It illustrates ELLs' feelings about their grades.
   D. It develops self-directed language learners.

   Answer: C. It illustrates ELLs' feelings about their grades.

   Administering self-assessment is valid in Options A, B, and D. Feelings about grades are not a valid reason to administer the test, so C is the correct response.

93. **Which of the following criteria should NOT be included in an oral evaluation of ELLs?**
(Average) (Skill 12.3)

   A. Reading a dialogue.
   B. Accuracy.
   C. Telling a story.
   D. Asking for clarification.

   Answer: A. Reading a dialogue.

   Reading aloud is troublesome for even the most skilled native speaker. It is not a valid way to evaluate oral production of ELLs.

94. **Which of the following tasks is a valid reading evaluation of ELLs?**
(Average) (Skill 12.4)

   A. Multiple choice questions.
   B. Open-ended questions.
   C. Completing a text with information based on class work.
   D. Information transfer.

   Answer: D. Information transfer.

   An information transfer exercise (e.g., reading a text and summarizing it in graphic form) requires the ELL to understand what he or she is reading and to rephrase it for placement in a graph.

95. **Which of the following tasks could be included in a writing evaluation of ELLs?**
(Average) (Skill 12.5)

A. Multiple choice questions.
B. Reading a dialogue and answering questions.
C. Responding to information given.
D. Cloze summaries.

Answer: C. Responding to information given.

By posing a task for the ELL, the ESOL teacher is engaging the ELL in a practical or informative writing process (e.g., answering a letter of complaint sent in by a customer).

96. **Which of the following methods could be used to evaluate ELLs in content area material?**
(Average) (Skill 12.6)

A. Multiple choice.
B. True-false.
C. Essays.
D. Exhibits or projects.

Answer: D. Exhibits or projects.

Options A, B, and C may be challenging for ELLs who have poor language skills. However, using exhibits or projects can show their learning even if they have trouble expressing themselves in English.

97. **Which of the following activities would encourage authentic oral language production in ELLs?**
(Average) (Skill 13.1)

A. Group work.
B. Oral quizzes.
C. One-on-one interviews with teacher.
D. Oral reports.

Answer: A. Group work.

Options B, C, and D can be stressful for any student, but especially an ELL who is concerned about his or her language skills. However, group work permits the ELLs to work with their peers toward a common goal and encourages the use of authentic language in a relaxed atmosphere.

98. **Which of the following activities is probably the most meaningful for developing ELL's communicative skills?**
(Rigorous) (Skill 13.2)

A. Cloze procedure activities.
B. Gap-filling activities.
C. Role plays and skits.
D. TPR.

Answer: C. Role plays and skits.

Options A and B are written activities and would not contribute to communicative competence. TPR is a listening exercise. Option C is the best option for developing the ability to communicate in a "spontaneous" form.

99. **Which of the following instructions is appropriate for introducing a listening exercise to ELLs?**
(Average) (Skill 13.3)

A. Introducing the dialog with "Listen to the passage…".
B. Presenting a speaker by stating his name and to whom he is related to in the class.
C. Stating the context of the passage being presented.
D. Assigning five questions to be answered during the listening process by stating that they are a quiz.

Answer: C. Stating the context of the passage being presented.

By stating the context of the listening exercise, the ESOL teacher is activating previous knowledge of this type of task and of similar situations.

100. **Which one of the following activities would be the best option for teaching stress in speech?**
(Easy) (Skill 13.4)

A. Have students listen to a text being read and follow the stress patterns marked in the textbook.
B. Have students beat out the rhythm while listening to a text.
C. Have students silently read a text and mark the stressed words.
D. Explain the rules for stress in words and sentences in English.

Answer: B. Have students beat out the rhythm while listening to a text.

Option D is ineffective unless dealing with older learners who request this information. Options A and C engage the learner in actively increasing his or her skills in recognizing and utilizing the stress patterns of English. Still, utilizing the natural instinct of humans to move when listening to rhythms, beating out a rhythm is often the best option for the majority of students, especially children and teens who love music or are musically inclined.

101. **When the teacher is correcting a student's speech, the teacher should:**
(Easy) (Skill 13.4)

A. Carefully correct all mistakes.
B. Consider the context of the error.
C. Confirm the error by repeating it.
D. Repeat the student's message but correcting it.

Answer: D. Repeat the student's message but correcting it.

Both A and C are inappropriate at all times. Option B should always be considered by the ESOL teacher, but does not lead to correction. Thus, Option D is the most appropriate option.

102. **Which of the following types of correction is appropriate?**
(Easy) (Skill 14.1)

A. Lexical correction.
B. Correcting sentence semantic errors.
C. Correction of overgeneralization.
D. Correction of simplification errors.

Answer: A. Lexical correction.

Students, in general, resent teachers who correct their papers by putting red marks all over the paper. A better approach is to decide on specific problem areas to be corrected in all papers (e.g., the incorrect use of connectors). Thus, Options B, C, and D would not be effective methods of correcting student papers. Option A, correcting lexis, is generally accepted by ELLs.

103. **When correcting written work, what is the most effective way for the teacher to correct the paper of her ELLs?**
(Easy) (Skill 14.1)

A. Correct all vocabulary errors.
B. Correct some grammatical errors.
C. Correct all errors.
D. Correct one example of different types of errors.

Answer: D. Correct one example of different types of errors.

See explanation for Question 42.

104. **Which of the following options is probably the most beneficial to ELLs who do not yet read in their native language?**
(Easy) (Skill 14.2)

   A. Instruction based on needs.
   B. Involving the ELL's family.
   C. Oral storytelling in the classroom.
   D. Using the same methods of instruction as used for native speakers.

Answer: A. Instruction based on needs.

ELLs who do not read in their native language may come from societies where storytelling or other oral traditions are used. They may have not had the privilege of going to school because of conflicts in the area where they lived. Some worked to increase the family income, or lived in rural areas where there were no schools. Their first school experience may be in the U.S., so instruction based upon each child's specific needs will probably be the most successful option when dealing with these situations.

105. **Which of the following ESL goals is achieved when having ELLs retell a story?**
(Easy) (Skill 14.3)

   A. ELLs are better able to understand the culture of the story.
   B. ELLs obtain practice in recognizing important story elements.
   C. ELLs are able to incorporate some of the language of the story in their speech.
   D. ELLs derive esthetic pleasure from the story.

Answer: C. ELLs are able to incorporate some of the language of the story in their speech.

Retelling of stories provides the teacher with insight into the student's comprehension of the story as well as their ability to use the structure of the story to retain and organize information. It is a pre-step to summarizing.

106. **What is the best option for beginning reading instruction for ELLs who have reached the level of speech emergence in their native language? (Average) (Skill 14.4)**

    A. Reading instruction should be delayed until the ELL has mastered the oral language of his native language.
    B. Reading instruction should be begun after one year in the U.S. school system where the ELL received oral English language instruction.
    C. Reading instruction should be begun in the ELL's L1.
    D. All ELLs benefit from beginning reading instruction in L2.

    Answer: D. All ELLs benefit from beginning reading instruction in L2.

    Current theory suggests that all ELLs benefit from beginning reading instruction in L2. This is supported by the problems of having a nation with large populations of immigrants from diverse countries and language groups which strain school budgets when trying to provide for L1 instruction. Then, too, many theorists believe that since academic language needs five to seven years to develop, ELLs need to be provided with early reading to reduce this gap.

107. **Which of the following writing traits are illustrated in the passage which follows? (Rigorous) (Skill 14.5)**

    Writing passage: "My country is beautiful. I love my country very much. My mother love my country."

    A. Fluency: Beginning Level, Sentence Variety: Beginning Level.
    B. Fluency: Intermediate Level, Vocabulary: Intermediate Level.
    C. Grammar: Beginning Level, Organization: Intermediate Level.
    D. Grammar: Intermediate Level, Genre: Intermediate Level.

    Answer: A. Fluency: Beginning Level, Sentence Variety: Beginning Level.

    Careful analysis of the paragraph demonstrates a beginning fluency level (student is able to write a few short sentences) and a beginning level of vocabulary (may need to ask for translation).

108. **Which one of the following is a negative result of instructing children in their first language?**
(Average) (Skill 15.1)

A. Instruction in L1 lowers the affective filter.
B. L1 instruction clarifies misunderstandings in L2.
C. L1 instruction can be used to explain differences in L1 and L2.
D. ELLs can become dependent upon L1 instruction.

Answer: D. ELLs can become dependent upon L1 instruction.

Instruction in L1 has many positive variables, such as those listed in Options A, B, and C. Option D is a hindrance when instructing ELLs if they become dependent on their native or heritage language.

109. **Which one of the following is NOT a step in the Language Experience Approach?**
(Average) (Skill 15.2)

A. The ELL retells a personal story.
B. While writing the story down, the teacher makes minor grammar corrections.
C. The ELL reads his or her story.
D. The students illustrate or dramatize the story.

Answer: B. While writing the story down, the teacher makes minor grammar corrections.

Language Experience Stories are those that students tell the teacher, who writes exactly what is told to her. Spelling and punctuation should be correct, but grammatical structure should not be changed. This method demonstrates to students that their language can be written down and read by others. It is an empowering experience for beginning readers—and especially ELLs.

110. **Which one of the following does NOT represent a beginning reading development technique?**
(Average) (Skill 15.3)

  A. Holding up the left hand in order to remember which side of the text to begin reading first.
  B. Memorizing sight words.
  C. Learning sentence structure patterns.
  D. Memorizing vocabulary lists.

  Answer: D. Memorizing vocabulary lists.

  Options A, B, and C are all beginning reading development techniques; Option D is not.

111. **Which of the following is NOT a reading comprehension skill?**
(Average) (Skill 15.4)

  A. Skimming.
  B. Scanning.
  C. Restating.
  D. Describing.

  Answer: D. Describing.

  Options A, B, and C are all reading comprehension techniques; Option D is not.

112. **Which of the following is NOT an academic writing skill?**
(Average) (Skill 15.5)

  A. Planning the paper.
  B. Doing research.
  C. Quick-writing the paper.
  D. Revising.

  Answer: C. Quick-writing the paper.

  Options A, B, and D are all factors in the academic writing process; Option C is not. Option C is used to get students to reflect on what they learned in class in a low pressure way. It should not be graded or assessed.

113. **Which of the following is an important skill that ELLs entering the U.S. school system in middle or high school will probably not possess even if they are fairly skilled in academic writing?**
(Average) (Skill 15.6)

A. Using dictionaries.
B. Using advanced vocabulary.
C. Writing in different genres.
D. Using connectors.

Answer: C. Writing in different genres.

Options A, B, and D are all writing skills that most middle to high school students possess, including ELLs. Option C is not a skill that would be expected of an ELL encountering English and U.S. schooling for the first time. Building up academic writing skills is a process that takes time and unless the ELL has had the privilege of attending American schools abroad or schools offering International Baccalaureate Programs, it is unlikely that they would have been exposed to the different genres of academic English.

114. **When addressing school-age ELLs who do not read in their heritage language, which one of the following is the LEAST appropriate action?**
(Rigorous) (Skill 16.1)

A. Introducing topics such as life survival skills.
B. Having them read authentic materials such as menus.
C. Using the Language Experience Approach.
D. Using CALLA.

Answer: A. Introducing topics such as life survival skills.

Options B, C, and D are all appropriate actions or teaching methods appropriate to address the problem of illiteracy in L1 and have been used successfully in the ESOL classroom. Introducing topics such as life survival skills might be appropriate to adult learners, but for children, more academic themes would probably serve their needs better.

115. **Which one of the following is the LEAST appropriate strategy for activating prior knowledge and relating it to the content-area objectives in the English classroom?**
(Rigorous) (Skill 16.2)

A. Creating "All about Me" autobiographies.
B. Using dialogue journals with the ELLs.
C. Discussing themes such as "Family Origins".
D. Having Q and A sessions with the ELL about home culture.

Answer: D. Having Q and A sessions with the ELL about home culture.

Options A, B, and C are all techniques for activating prior knowledge in a non-threatening way; Option D is not. Option D might make some ELLs feel pressure and anxiety.

116. **Which one of the following is NOT the most appropriate option to make content-area lessons accessible to ELLs?**
(Easy) (Skill 16.3)

A. Using vocabulary lists from the text.
B. Speaking loudly so that they understand.
C. Reading the story/text and checking for comprehension constantly.
D. Writing new vocabulary words, expressions or idioms on the white board.

Answer: B. Speaking loudly so that they understand.

Options A and D are all good options for scaffolding vocabulary. Option C is a way to check for comprehension. Option B is used by many in an effort to communicate with foreigners. It is ineffective because many foreigners simply do not understand what is being said; they are not hard of hearing. Indeed, in many cultures, raising the voice is considered uncouth and therefore offensive.

117. **When bringing ELLs up to grade level, which of the following is the most appropriate option for the ESOL teacher?**
(Rigorous) (Skill 16.4)

A. Teach according to curriculum.
B. Select high-priority concepts for instruction.
C. Instruct the ELL in appropriate language skills.
D. Concentrate on pronunciation and listening skills.

Answer: B. Select high-priority concepts for instruction.

The ESOL teacher must bring ELLs up to grade-level as soon as possible. Otherwise, ELLs lose precious time in acquiring academic English and the content which is taught at each level. Therefore, the ESOL teacher should strive for major concepts in addition to the skills and processes associated with them. In other words, the ESOL instructor should aim for profundity and not breadth of content.

118. **Which one of the following is NOT a tenet of CALLA?**
(Rigorous) (Skill 16.5)

A. In mathematics, science, etc., grade level should determine content.
B. ELLs can gradually learn the specific language of the subject area.
C. Encourage ELLs to use higher level cognitive processes.
D. Reading in L2 can be postponed until oral language is developed.

Answer: D. Reading in L2 can be postponed until oral language is developed.

Options A, B, and C are all tenets of CALLA; Option D is not. Postponing reading in ELLs is a disservice to their learning process.

119. **Which of the following options is NOT a cognitive learning strategy?**
(Rigorous) (Skill 4.4.6)

A. Note taking.
B. Ordering.
C. K-W-L charts.
D. Classifying.

Answer: A. Note taking.

Only Option A is not a cognitive learning strategy.

120. **Which of the following options would best serve ELLs in learning about the library?**
(Average) (Skill 16.7)

A. A tour and introduction by the librarian.
B. A text on the library followed by comprehension exercises
C. A gap-filling exercise on the library.
D. A quiz on the library.

Answer: C. A gap-filling exercise on the library.

Engaging ELLs actively in learning about the library and its services through a "Treasure Hunt" activity, an information-gap exercise, or some other task will help them remember the material much better than a tour and lecture, a reading text, or a quiz.

CONSTRUCTED RESPONSE   **ASSIGNMENT ONE**

Use the information below to complete the assignment that follows.

Developing knowledge and skills in English semantics is an essential component of learning English as a new language.

- Describe one instructional strategy that an ESOL teacher could use to promote an English Language Learner's development of knowledge and skills in English semantics.

- Explain why the strategy would be effective in their development of English as a new language.

RESPONSE SHEET FOR CONSTRUCTED RESPONSE ASSIGNMENT ONE

When discussing sentence semantics, we are referring to how the elements of the sentence hold together to create meaning. One strategy for helping ELLs achieve competency in meaning would be to demonstrate how sentences are built from basic words into more complex sentences. The teacher writes a minimal sentence on the board, such as: She gives him an apple. The teacher then has students insert an appropriate word in the sentence where there is a caret. If the student's word is inappropriate, the teacher mimes to the other students asking them if the word is correct. If it isn't , the teacher erases the word and the activity continues.

English Language Learners often have difficulty in understanding how to amplify and vary their sentences when writing or speaking. The purpose of the activity is to encourage beginners to learn about the word order in sentences. The strategy described would be effective because it is a "free" or open-ended activity requiring the English Language Learner to use his or her cognitive processes in addition to knowledge of the English language.

CONSTRUCTED RESPONSE   **ASSIGNMENT TWO**

Use the information below to complete the assignment that follows.

The process of culture shock can be difficult for most English Language Learning students.

- Describe one strategy an ESOL instructor can use to support the ELL in the process of culture shock.

- Explain why the strategy would be effective.

RESPONSE SHEET FOR CONSTRUCTED RESPONSE ASSIGNMENT TWO

One strategy an ESOL teacher can use to support English Language Learners suffering from culture shock would be to assign another student of the same language background to be the buddy of the newly arrived student. Since each school has its own rules about how to line up, how to ask for food, or how and where to sit, it is intimidating for newcomers to face these obstacles alone.

This strategy would be effective in supporting a newly arrived English Language Learner and promoting feelings of safety and security. By helping the new student to overcome the anxieties of the first days in the new school, the ESOL teacher is helping the English Language Learner work through the hostility stage of culture shock. As the student develops more coping mechanisms by reducing his or her anxiety, the student will be able to focus more on learning.

CONSTRUCTED RESPONSE

ASSIGNMENT THREE

Use the information below to complete the assignment that follows.

There are a variety of instructional methodologies and approaches ESOL teachers can use to assess the English Language Learner's progress in English besides standardized testing.

- Describe one instructional setting (i.e., individual student, small group, or whole class), including language-proficiency level of student(s), and a situation in which it would be appropriate for an ESOL teacher to use an alternative assessment.

- Explain why this alternative assessment would be an effective way to assess the ELL. Be sure to include information about specific features of the assessment and its characteristics or goals to support your explanation.

RESPONSE SHEET FOR CONSTRUCTED RESPONSE ASSIGNMENT THREE

> One setting and situation for using alternative assessment of an English Language Learner (ELL) would be to accurately evaluate the learning of the student over a period of time using a portfolio. A case in point would be an ELL who is newly arrived in the United States school system and does not yet have sufficient reading or writing skills to make standardized or regular classroom testing possible.
>
> In the case of this student, all the teachers involved in instructing the student can include samples of the student's work. Thus, writing samples, mathematics problems, and science papers can be included. Other information can be obtained from teacher assessment and self-assessments made by the student. These portfolios should reflect the learning goals of the student. Using criteria such as rubrics or checklists can be used to show the level of achievement
>
> --or the lack of it.

CONSTRUCTED RESPONSE   **ASSIGNMENT FOUR**

Use the information below to complete the assignment that follows.

ESOL teachers use a variety of strategies to promote English Language Learners' written language development.

- Describe one instructional strategy that an ESOL teacher could use to promote an English Language Learner's development of writing academic papers in science.

- Explain why the strategy you described would be effective in developing the ELL's academic writing.

RESPONSE SHEET FOR CONSTRUCTED RESPONSE ASSIGNMENT FOUR

One instructional strategy that an ESOL teacher could use to develop academic writing in science would be to guide the students in the process of discovering causes and effects through eliciting answers to questions and rephrasing their answers with the appropriate language of cause and effect (e.g. A force acts upon this object, since, this allows/permits, etc.). The ESOL instructor can list appropriate terms in a word ladder for the students to refer to as they compose their papers.

This strategy is a simple yet effective one because it models the correct phrasing of cause and effect in scientific writing. As the ESOL teacher elicits more and more information about the topic from the ELLs, they are learning to think more deeply about the topic and see that there is often more than one cause and effect. By facilitating the appropriate language, the teacher enables ELLs to use the appropriate phrases in their writing.

XAMonline, Inc.
25 First Street, Suite 106
Cambridge, MA 02141
P: 1-800-509-4128
F: 617-583-5552

2010

www.XAMonline.com

Georgia Tests for Educator Licensure GACE

PO#:	Store/School:		
Address 1:			
Address 2:			
City, State, Zip:			
Credit Card #:		Exp:	
Phone		Fax:	
Email			

ISBN	TITLE	Qty	Retail	Total
978-1-58197-257-3	Basic Skills 200, 201, 202		$28.95	
978-1-58197-773-8	Biology 026, 027		$59.95	
978-1-58197-584-0	Science 024, 025		$59.95	
978-1-60787-062-3	English 020, 021		$59.95	
978-1-60787-060-9	Educational Leadership 173, 174		$59.95	
978-1-58197-896-8	Physics 030, 031		$59.95	
978-1-58197-531-4	Art Education Sample Test 109, 110		$15.00	
978-1-58197-545-1	History 034, 035		$59.95	
978-1-58197-774-5	Health and Physical Education 115, 116		$59.95	
978-1-58197-540-6	Chemistry 028, 029		$59.95	
978-1-58197-534-5	Reading 117, 118		$59.95	
978-1-58197-724-0	Media Specialist 101, 102		$59.95	
978-1-58197-535-2	Middle Grades Reading 012		$59.95	
978-1-58197-591-8	Middle Grades Science 014		$59.95	
978-1-58197-345-7	Middle Grades Mathematics 013		$59.95	
978-1-58197-686-1	Middle Grades Social Science 015		$59.95	
978-158-197-598-7	Middle Grades Language Arts 011		$59.95	
978-1-58197-346-4	Mathematics 022, 023		$59.95	
978-1-58197-549-9	Political Science 032, 033		$59.95	
978-1-58197-588-8	Paraprofessional Assessment 177		$59.95	
978-1-58197-589-5	Professional Pedagogy Assessment 171, 172		$28.95	
978-1-60787-064-7	Early Childhood Education 001, 002		$59.95	
978-1-58197-587-1	School Counseling 103, 104		$59.95	
978-1-58197-720-2	Spanish 141, 142		$59.95	
978-1-58197-610-6	Special Education General Curriculum 081, 082		$73.50	
978-1-58197-530-7	French Sample Test 143, 144		$15.00	
978-1-60787-061-6	Early Childhood Special Education 004		$59.95	
			SUBTOTAL	
	1 book $8.70, 2 books $11.00. 3+ books $15.00		Ship	
			TOTAL	

CPSIA information can be obtained at www.ICGtesting.com
Printed in the USA
BVOW09s1147101115

426550BV00005B/192/P

9 781607 870630